Love, Freedom, and Wellness:

A Guide to Living an Empowered Life

Marla Friedman, PhD, CN

Integrative Wellness
Glen Head, NY

3 1571 00321 6903

Integrative Wellness Publishing, a division of The Center for Integrative Wellness
1005 Glen Cove Ave.
Glen Head, NY 11545

ISBN-13: 978-0615983790
ISBN-10: 0615983790

Design by Sharon Shiraga

Dedication

To my family, my patients,
and the human potential to love, overcome, and heal.

Acknowledgments

First of all, I'd like to thank my darling husband, Eddie, who supported and believed in me every step of the way, as well as my precious sons and family, who have provided much love and encouragement for this project. I'm also very grateful for the love that lives on inside me from my family and loved ones who have passed.

Thank you to Nicole K. Miller, my book midwife, editor, wise friend and advisor, for her patience and talent for taking me from practitioner to author; Coleen Higgins for her multiple skills, her loyal and ongoing support, and for being such a fine human being; The Viktor Frankl Institute, which has become a meaningful part of my work in helping people overcome adversity; and Kripalu Yoga Center and Canyon Ranch for providing such peaceful spaces for writing retreats.

To all my friends and colleagues who have been excited by, and supportive of, my writing journey; and to my friends, colleagues, and the directors of Hippocrates Health Institute, where I finished my book in a vitalizing, pure, inspired environment. I'm grateful for the Institute for Functional Medicine, for their wonderful training and education that continues to deepen my understanding of the underlying causes of suffering and illness, in order to get the bigger picture. I'm thankful to the American Academy of Anti-Aging Medicine for their wonderful Fellowship Program, and the valuable learning and life-long friends that have come from it, and to all of my life teachers, from the fields of psychology, spirituality, and nutrition, who have contributed to my journey of integrating these elements in my own life and work.

Table of Contents

Introduction

My Message of Hope

Our minds have great power over everything we do. Our beliefs, our emotions, and our attitudes impact how we interact with life. These aspects of our selves carry great influence over our health and nutritional behaviors. Though these behaviors may seem unchangeable to us, they are, in truth, fluid. Constructive, wisdom-filled thinking can change our health actions, and culminate in balanced body chemistry and greater resilience to stress. Contrastingly, acting out negative emotions on the body results in poor self-care, low self-esteem, and deficient nutrition. The consequences of these actions are far-reaching into the quality of our lives, and can lead to depression, anxiety, low energy, and illness. When people think about changing their nutrition, they believe it will be hard. They fear they will suffer deprivation, frustration, and defeat; but that is a false belief.

My message of hope, is that real, lasting change is possible, and begins with looking inside ourselves; healing our conflicts, self-defeating thoughts, and behaviors. As we integrate psychological growth and empowered nutrition, we become in alignment with our true selves. This mobilizes positive action, awakening to the realization of our true health goals, which affect every aspect of our lives. Our body, mind, and spirit want to heal. Overcoming our challenges helps us to grow as human beings, with greater love and compassion for our selves and others.

Love, Freedom, and Wellness

Chapter One

"Love is the only sane and satisfactory answer
to the problem of human existence."
—Erich Fromm

Why Love?

Love, freedom, and wellness are powerful words; within them they carry the potential to bring meaning to one's life. They came to me as the title of my book because they are each essential, interlocking parts that have a profound synergy in our lives. Love is the most powerful force in the universe, something we all long for in all aspects of life, from our earliest infanthood to our oldest age. Love is an intensely personal force that we desire from others, but one that we also need to give to ourselves. Without this precious life-giving element, we suffer. It is often the elusive truth behind why we don't take better care of ourselves. This lack of inner love is not often so obvious to us. There are many people, no matter how intelligent they are, who do not realize why they consistently sabotage themselves. The process may originate through a lack of self-care, and the consequences of those actions, and then intensify with the repetitive cycle of doing great for a little while, and then not. As an example of this sabotage, many people lose weight and then gain it back again, and a primary reason for this is often that they have not yet seen the elusive and hidden chasm in their relationship with themselves.

Love is not about destructive self-indulgence without boundaries, which is often an attempt to overcompensate for the lack of love inside us. We fill up again and again with something that leaves us empty and longing for the next round. Developing the capacity to direct love toward our self is an element that nothing can replace. There is no real substitute except the real thing: loving self-care, humility, self-respect, and self-honor. Loving self-care has to do with how we treat, how we speak to, and the true feelings we have toward ourselves. Love, or the lack of it, affects every decision we make, and how we allow others to treat us.

Loving self-care is like having protection in a safe harbor, rather than being vulnerable and exposed to the harsh elements of life on the open seas. It is crucial to learn how to set healthy boundaries that perhaps you've never set before.

> "Unconditional Love is the most powerful
> stimulant of the immune system.
> The truth is: love heals."
> —Dr. Bernie Siegel

There is an endless supply of LOVE in the world. It is possible, even if you do not love yourself enough yet, that you can learn to connect with yourself in a new way; one that manifests through compassion, empathy, the teachings available to you on your life journey, and a realization of true meaning and purpose. Opening your heart to love helps you to see what is truly important in your life, and in the lives of others who you may know, or may not know, where you can make a huge difference. This concept might be philosophically familiar already, but to live it may be a new reality for you. Finding the missing piece of you that is unhealed and hidden away, the vital connection you have been longing for, and integrating it, will create a new, balanced, inspired ground to live your life from. What gets in the way of loving yourself and treating yourself well? **DON'T MISS THIS MESSAGE!** This can be the paradigm shift that will help you put everything you are dealing with into a wiser perspective.

This book starts with love and ends with love. You, the reader, can choose to embrace this precious element with great power and meaning, in a way that connects us to ourselves, to others, and to life.

Why Freedom?

It humbles me to write about freedom. Freedom has such an immense power, one that is needed on this earth in infinite ways. Humans need the freedom of having their basic needs met, whether it is the freedom to have shelter and safety, freedom from abuse of all kinds, freedom to have their human rights honored, freedom from hunger of all kinds. Millions of adults and children face this each day. We all need to help this change. Though part of our own personal freedom is to find a way of contributing to the world, with all its needs for help, this book focuses on our personal and internal freedoms:

- Freedom of choice in our attitudes, thoughts, actions, and behaviors.
- Freedom to express our freedom wisely, in a way that brings goodness to our lives and to the world.
- Freedom to be well, and to take steps to improve our physical and emotional health.
- Freedom from addiction and the ability to seek all the help and recovery that is available for us to save our life.
- Freedom to make ourselves a better person; one who is more caring, more related, and grateful for all the gifts we have.
- Freedom to realize our power and to use it for good.
- Freedom to fulfill our potential, and realize our goals and dreams for a meaningful life.
- Freedom in which we have self-respect for the commitments we have made and follow through on them.
- Freedom to make new decisions, choose our attitude, our behavior, and the life path we will take.

- Freedom to make a difference in the world, and to make it better in at least one way.
- Freedom to heal and connect with what is truly important to us.
- Freedom to reflect, and face when we get off-track.
- Freedom to tell ourselves the truth.
- Freedom to make amends, and to be truly sorry, in words and actions, for the ways we have hurt others.
- Freedom to choose a healthier path, step by step, with love, help, and support.
- Freedom within, developing the power of awareness in you.
- Freedom to move from powerless to empowered; there is something you can do about it.

Looking at the list, what freedoms are you missing in your life, and what would you like to become free of?

Why Wellness?

Wellness is the optimal balance of mind, body, and spirit. The term "wellness" is used a lot these days, and though it is greatly desired, it is not always truly understood and embraced. Embracing wellness is a proactive process of learning, one in which we develop a willingness to change the crucial facets of our lives where they are needed. When we enter the wellness continuum, it is never too late to begin to work wherever you are.

Wellness includes different facets:

1. **Emotional health:** Love in action, becoming more aware, healing and resolving, and improving our relationship with self and others.
2. **Spiritual health:** Our quest for meaning and purpose, being intrigued with the unfolding mystery of life, connecting with higher wisdom, and cultivating hope, joy, humility, courage, gratitude, and truth.
3. **Nutritional and biochemical wellness:** Improving our nutrition and

lifestyle, implementing prevention practices, transforming our lives, and committing to self-care and to greater wellness.

4. **Physical movement:** Strengthening our body and fitness level with physical exercise, enlivening our sexuality, and improving sleep quality and sleep hygiene.

5. **Social wellness:** Our connection to community, our friends, our causes, having fun, enjoying leisure activities, music, and celebrations with others.

6. **Intellectual:** Curiosity, creativity, life-long learning, continual development of your mind and knowledge, and openness to new ideas.

7. **Occupational:** Approaching your life's work with a new attitude, learning new skills, and growing and developing in new abilities that are fulfilling.

Your wellness is greatly determined by your beliefs, and your lifestyle choices are the most impactful and significant factors affecting your health and wellbeing.

So Let's Begin...

Are you struggling?
If so, in what ways have you been struggling?
How much mental and emotional energy is being consumed
by troubling thoughts about your appearance,
your health, your weight, or your life?

How we answer these questions is part of our personal journey of Love, Freedom, and Wellness. This book discusses the elements we need to truly integrate into our psyche in order to lead an empowered and healthy life. What are Love, Freedom, and Wellness, and how do they fit together?

Achieving lasting wellness involves psychological, emotional, nutritional, and spiritual healing. It involves all aspects of us, not just any one facet. There is a psychology of nutrition. It is very personal, as it is our own unique way of thinking and feeling that leads to the way we are living. Often we want to change, but we get bogged down and stuck in the actions that do not serve us. No matter what we think we know, our psychology trumps our behavior every time when it comes to self-care and wellness. Our minds are capable of incredible dances of thought designed by us to meet some illusive inner demands hiding just under our conscious intentions. We want to do better for ourselves, but those hidden facets of our being can sabotage us as we consciously decide to change. We meet this attempt to change with our own resistances, rationalizations, and procrastination. The key to healing is by gaining insight and understanding into this deeper part of our self, which tells us that healing and support is needed. People often say to me, "I don't know what happened! I *found myself* eating the very thing I know is bad for me and makes me ill." Imagine that! They found themselves doing something unconsciously! How does that happen, and how can we begin to become more aware, and transform those hidden patterns in order to gain the freedom to create a healthier, more vibrant life?

This book is an exploration of those unknown parts of us that play havoc with our sense of wellness, and sabotage our best efforts to heal ourselves. We need to look at what is unhealed within, that which needs new awareness and healing attention from us. In my opinion, this is why, with all the information we now know about health and wellbeing, we still struggle with taking care of ourselves. We need to bring light to what we do not yet see, and have that be our foundation for the new understanding and healing that is greatly needed. This newfound awareness can bring real hope, because it exposes never before faced inner frontiers of possibility for us to connect with our deeper selves, which are often crying for attention.

Those deeper selves demand that a path be created in order to empower us to treat ourselves with love, self-respect, and honor. As we learn to do so, our life transforms.

As a Psychotherapist and Clinical Nutritionist, I work with the deeply intimate association between the mind and body, embracing the varied and complex issues that we have as human beings. Many of my patients come in with interpersonal concerns needing psychotherapy, such as depression, anxiety, mood disorders, relationship and marital issues, addictions, co-dependency, emotional and compulsive eating, and other eating disorders. They also come to see me for nutrition and lifestyle-related help, such as developing a life program for their weight issues, a nutritional program for Type II diabetes, metabolic syndrome, cardiovascular problems, autoimmune conditions, gut issues, food allergies, and migraines. In each instance, they are longing for someone to treat the whole person and not just one isolated issue. Human beings are very complex, and we need and deserve to be understood and honored by the practitioners that treat us, so that we feel cared for and empowered to understand ourselves more deeply. Often when a person goes into a traditional medical situation, they may spend a short time with the doctor and then the prescription pad comes out. People then drive home with their prescriptions and look up the side effects, wondering about the effect this drug will have on their body. Alternatively, a patient may hear from their doctor, "You've got to lose weight," but the doctor doesn't have the time to go any further with it. The office visit is not really set up to get to deeply know this person sitting in front of them: their life stressors, their thinking, fears, need for support, their traumas, and complicated health histories, emotional history, and addictions, which takes time. I believe there is a greater need for patients to be seen and understood as a whole being. Instead, the doctor addresses the symptoms being presented, and not the whole synergistic being. But, everything in us is connected.

They may ask the doctor if there is something that they can do with diet and nutrition to help them with illnesses and are often told that, "It has nothing to do with that;" even oncologists often don't ask people what they eat, though there has been much research on the connection between nutrition and cancer. This brings to mind Dr. Bernie Siegel's book, *Love, Medicine, and Miracles,* where he describes the moment that he realized he did not know his patients as whole people, and he began asking them questions about their lives. Many miracles came out of that epiphany.

My patients often come to me already on numerous pharmaceuticals. They arrive at my office, hopeful to finally share their story and be truly heard. In a space of honoring and honesty, I listen and tune into this person for the next hour and a half, with no interruptions, so that I can begin to fully understand all the aspects of who they are. This will often lead to the integral question, "What else can I do to improve my health?"

I so respect and appreciate that this question can open the door to more powerful life-changing possibilities. It is my pleasure to offer benign, non-invasive solutions that have the potential to bring relief, both physically and emotionally, and help my patients begin to improve their health from this very first meeting. Their healing journey has begun!

It is also natural for this process to bring up resistances as we learn how to change our thinking. People need a practical "working through" process. They often need nutritional counseling and psychotherapy in order to change their behaviors and bring about lasting results in both psychological and bio-chemical changes. They need to heal the underlying emotional conflict that gets played out on the innocent body. This necessity is often greatly overlooked.

Many people are in quiet desperation over this struggle with themselves and their health. This underlying suffering and its causes are not valued or addressed often enough in our society, which often leaves people feeling very alone with this inner battle. There is an epidemic of people beating themselves up. They do it so automatically that they often do not even realize that this is destructive behavior and a problem. People often talk to themselves in a way that they would never dare to talk to other people. They are used to talking internally this way and it seems normal. But it's not. By learning and practicing compassion for one's self and others, we lay the groundwork for a deeper healing process.

This book is intended to bring awareness and inspiration in order to help you honor your body, rather than punish yourself. It provides strategies for healing the internal struggle, and life affirming insights for you to internalize, with guidelines that serve you in this process, and give you a safe harbor for your emotional relationship with yourself and your unique challenges. They become part of you and set you free.

What would freedom from this struggle actually look like? There is a space in which we can live where we can have peace with our selves, our body, and our emotions, and even if that sounds amazing or unbelievable, this work is an attempt to create that space for you. This space is available to you, even if you didn't even know it existed. This program creates an inner paradigm shift to a new way of living that has the potential to set you free.

That freedom will enable you to not only achieve an ideal health and wellness level for you, but it can bring about a lasting healthy relationship with your inner self and with food, one that can stay with you for life. This also creates a foundation for whatever else needs healing. Once you've internalized a new behavioral and nutritional lifestyle, it is possible to keep the balance you've achieved with confidence, empowerment, and ease. It'll transform you inside and out and leave you with a better sense of who you really are.

My intentions with this book are to inspire and empower you. Let's go into the trenches together and begin the healing journey wherever you are in the process. Let's face it, open up to it, grieve it, change it, and heal it. No matter what you think, *change and healing are possible.*

My Journey to Wellness

Chapter Two

"Simply touching a difficult memory with some slight willingness to heal, begins to soften the holding and tension around it."
—Stephen Levine, *A Year to Live*

How I became involved in psychology, nutrition, and spirituality is a question I've pondered many times. I believe that my attraction to this field came out of a deep longing and desire to know that there was more to life than what appeared on the surface. I realize, looking back, that even from a young age, I was a seeker and wanted to find deeper meaning in life. I had this feeling that there were amazing hidden truths that only certain special people knew. I wanted to find these special people, these wise mentors, teachers, teachings, therapists, and trainings that would help me to expand and grow. And when I did, they indeed became profound teachers in my life.

Many years ago, I studied with Stephen Levine, a man of great wisdom and compassion. His life's work revolves around the emotional and spiritual support of the death and bereavement process. At one workshop I attended, that he did with his beautiful and very wise wife, Ondrea, he said that, "We need to make room in our own heart for our own pain, so we can be present and compassionate with other people's pain." I realize that this point is so deeply true, now more than ever. All people long for being treated with compassion and understanding. These qualities are often lacking in our relationship with ourselves, and in the interpersonal relationships we have with others. We need to learn how to give compassion to ourselves, and to develop the ability to receive it from others. Learning and incorporating compassion and empathy into our being is a developmental process that is necessary for our growth and true overall wellness.

I remember a sweet and poignant story I once heard from a rabbi. I'll paraphrase it for you: Before the world was created, G-d and the angels had a meeting to decide where to hide the holy light. Different angels offered their opinions on this. One suggested that they to hide it in the Vatican, where many seekers would come. Another suggested that they hide it on the highest mountaintop, and yet another thought to hide it away under the sea. Many other places were mentioned as well, because the angels figured that people would be searching everywhere for the light. Then the smallest angel got up, and said, "Let's hide the holy light inside man and woman, because it will be the last place they ever look." This story touched me and resonated deeply with my longing to find answers.

The massive, wisdom, love, and potential for growing awareness that lives inside us, is so profound; if only we could tap into this inner richness to find that golden light embedded within us that we often have forgotten about, or do not even know is there. One of the most endearing qualities of children is their immense creativity and their fresh insights and perceptions about life. Being in that creative and inspired place, is a sign of being connected to our innate aliveness.

But it's not always easy. Life is an incredible obstacle course in which we try to find our true selves, overcome our adversity, heal our wounds, become a better person, and become healthy emotionally, physically and spiritually. What a formidable challenge! As a child, I could sense the many the conflicts and hidden truths that surrounded me. I was always the kid who asked the questions that no one in my family wanted to ask. I wasn't intending to be irreverent; I didn't understand why I shouldn't be asking these questions. I was just truly curious and wanted answers. I didn't realize that answering depth-full questions isn't so easy for parents or others who have closed off certain aspects of themselves.

As an adolescent, I was drawn to psychotherapy. I loved my mother very deeply, and was concerned about how stressed and unnerved she often seemed to be feeling. At fourteen, I remember deciding that my mother definitely needed therapy. I called a doctor whose name I had once heard mentioned as a "nice man, and a caring doctor." I had no idea what kind of doctor he was, but figured that he could only help. I made an appointment to go speak to him and ask for his assistance in getting my mother into therapy. My parents didn't know I was doing this. I was really nervous.

I took numerous buses to get to Brooklyn to meet this doctor at his very old-fashioned office. When I arrived, I was shown into a very small consultation room. There were two examining rooms connected on each side of this room. While I waited nervously, a door to the other examining room directly in front of me, opened for a split second, and without trying to, I saw inside it. There, on the table, was a person in a medical gown, perched on all fours with his behind facing up in the air. In my momentary shock and bewilderment, I looked over to the doctor's desk and saw a huge book titled – Proctology! I gasped. Then I had the crushing realization that I had gone to speak to a proctologist when I really needed a psychologist. I thought of trying to escape the office before the doctor came in to see me. But during the few minutes I had to wait for the doctor to meet with me, I had somewhat recovered from my shock and figured that I had to make the best of it, and maybe he knew someone who could still help. I remember thinking *Oh no! I went to the wrong end to get my mother into therapy!*

I did end up speaking with the doctor that day who, as I think back, looked puzzled at the prospect of dealing with a fourteen-year-old girl asking to help get her mother into therapy. The conversation didn't last very long and he did attempt to help. He ended up speaking to my father, which prompted my father to speak briefly to me about it. My mom never ended up going into therapy. Looking back, what I found intriguing about this experience is that, at that time, I had had no direct experience with therapy, nor did I even know anyone who'd ever been in therapy. I wonder now how I even knew that therapy was something that could significantly lead to greater and healthier emotional freedom for myself, and others.

On a deep intuitive level, therapy just made sense to me. This experience led to my own deep, ongoing, inner work on myself, which profoundly changed my life and proved essential to my lifelong wellness and wellbeing. I realized that my wish for my mother's psychological healing, and my wish for my other family members to go into therapy as well, was also a longing for my own psychological work, and came from a deep wish to have a healthier and happier family. I knew that something seemed not right with us, but I wasn't yet able to put that feeling and intuitive insight into words.

Eventually, I learned that good therapy is learning to see what you do not see about yourself, working it through, and integrating it into our being. This leads to an increase in our perception and awareness of ourselves, which, in turn, can bring us greater compassion and empathy for ourselves, and others. By learning and developing healthy boundaries, we begin to reflect deeper self-respect and self-knowledge.

As a teenager, when things upset me, it took me much longer to unravel my feelings, and some issues took years to understand and work through. I didn't feel secure, or think I was smart. Deep down, I felt worried and conflicted. There were things lurking underneath the surface of my family system, which were not being addressed, and those hidden things showed up in me in the form of low self-esteem and inner conflict. I needed someone who I could really talk to, who would give me important insight and feedback, and would help me understand what was really going on. I was sensing many issues that were happening in my family, and naïvely tried to bring them up. Unfortunately, this unintentionally made them feel uncomfortable, and I was certainly not validated for my perceptive insights. I had been intuitively picking up on things not being addressed in my family, and as I found out much later on, many of the things I had been thinking about turned out to be very accurate.

Developing this part of myself that was intuitive, through very deep ongoing excellent psychoanalytic psychotherapy, led to developing my ability to help others on their journey to overcome and heal the difficulties in their lives. I needed help with what to do with all of my unresolved feelings, and my need for emotional healing, as I caught on to the deeper concerns that were occurring before me in my family. I realize now, that the hardest part was to emotionally embrace what was confusing, painful, and difficult in my family, in myself, and in my life. I had a longing to be seen for what I had to offer inside, and needed to begin to discover the richness within me.

My wise psychoanalyst once told me, "Therapy is seeing what you don't see about yourself." The desire in me to develop the ability to see deeply and clearly, to grow, and to heal, has also led me to loving the field of psychology, and the potential for growth and healing that good therapy provides. Therapy gives us a chance to become who we truly are; to seek and find and realize our true potential. I am grateful I followed my heart and searched until I found someone who could really help me.

One of the painful challenges that I had growing up, was that I had an older brother who was neurologically and emotionally disturbed. He was always a loner, and the type of help he truly needed was not available to him at the time. I remember that he had many deficits, and continually expressed his difficulties with intense emotional anger. He had a clever sense of humor when he was younger, but sadly, as he got older and he continued to decline, life became much more difficult for him, and for everyone who had to deal with him. As my parents themselves became older and ill, they could no longer shield my brother, and he became even more lost and angry. I was left in charge of all the responsibilities of overseeing his life and his complex needs for care. He was furious that his little sister was left in charge, even though he was not competent to take care of himself. I was now facing numerous challenges emotionally, physically, and spiritually, dealing with all that life was asking of me.

My brother had been married, and had two very special daughters. My younger niece, Wendy, was born with hydrocephalus and had many serious health and learning difficulties right from the beginning of her life. She needed to have brain surgery at two weeks old, and a shunt was installed to regulate the cerebral fluid in her spine and her brain. Her development was very affected by her condition. She had slow milestones; she did not walk until she was four years old. The miraculous part of Wendy is that, in spite of all her difficulties, she was a loveable, darling, cuddly child with an amazingly sweet heart.

As she grew up, her struggles continued; she had problems with balance and fell easily. She had learning difficulties, and it was hard to find what community would best serve her socially, emotionally, and educationally.

When she was twenty-two, she was living in Florida with her mother, Ethel, who was now divorced from my brother. Sadly, Ethel, at the young age of fifty-two, had a massive stroke and passed away. Wendy's older sister Jackie, who is also a very sweet soul, was very close to her mother and sister, and she and I worked on many issues together in support of Wendy. I had to figure out a life plan for my darling, disabled, twenty-two-year-old niece, who needed and deserved so much. I had moved her up to New York, and she stayed with me for a while. I connected her with ACLD an organization for adults with learning disabilities, and other difficulties. I found an apartment for her, renting a part of someone's house, so she could be near the center. This worked for a time, and gave her structure and a social involvement while she worked very hard as a cashier at a pharmacy. It still breaks my heart to know that there were some very unkind young people who worked there with her who would make fun of her and her disabilities. The thought of it makes my blood boil at the cruelty and insensitivity that she endured.

This unfortunate situation, though, elicited in me the desire to help communities with special needs through psychology and nutrition, and assist in creating in the larger world, greater humanity for people with challenges. Wendy faced this pain, and had the great fortitude to keep working and trying. I remember on days that had the heaviest snowstorms, she would somehow make sure she still got to work. It always reminded how essential human compassion and respect is for anyone with disabilities and challenges. Her sister, Jackie, and I had many discussions over these years, trying to always figure out what Wendy might need next, and how we could resolve all the difficulties that always seemed to pop up. One thing Wendy did have was the gift of the freedom and ability to vocalize and communicate anything that was bothering her. Many late nights were spent on the phone going over her new litany of complaints, and Jackie and I were her "go to" people on a fairly consistent basis.

However, after nine years of overseeing Wendy's life, and honored to have her call me "Aunt Mom," Wendy passed away soon after a routine operation on her feet; one which was intentioned to help improve her walking. Before the funeral, I began receiving phone calls from a variety of people throughout the country who knew Wendy, people that I had never even heard of. One by one they all told me how much they loved Wendy, how they had met her, and that they were the person who Wendy called with all her problems. There were about ten calls in all. I was in shock! I thought Jackie and I were the only ones she reached out to, and I came to realize there were also many others.

When I gave the eulogy at her funeral, I said that my niece was a very successful person. I shared the story of all these loving, concerned people that had called me.

"She was the only person I know that had twelve people she could call everyday to tell them all her worries, woes, challenges, and successes, and have them welcome her with open arms," I said.

Everyone at her funeral laughed and cried as they listened to this story. Wendy was filled with love, and I believe that this is what bonded her with all of the people who loved and cared for her. She was also very affectionate and funny, and I recall that some of my most enjoyable conversations were with her. I will always remember how adorable she was, how loving and determined she was, no matter what challenges she had. She was a great teacher for me, and I hope to always honor the touching and brave life that she led.

I will eternally love and miss her, and I know Jackie feels the same way. Wendy is now our guardian angel.

Finding Balance

To be a balanced person, we need to be able to stand up for ourselves, set healthy boundaries, and not allow ourselves to be mistreated by the destructive behaviors of others. At times, life hands us huge challenges and difficulties and we have only two choices: let them overwhelm us or constructively deal with them. I had decided that one of my biggest goals was to be emotionally healthy, no matter what it took; little did I know at the time how much meaning this process would have in my life.

First, I had to get myself healthy (an ever-evolving, ongoing process), and then I had to find a pathway to making this my life's work. By embarking on this challenge, mixed with my longing for emotional health and growth, led to me deepening my compassion, empathy, and understanding about the difficulties of life that we all embrace in some way or other. My early journey of seeking help and wisdom helped me to creatively and compassionately help others grow; and later led me to enter the field as a psychotherapist.

As a long time therapist, I have been witness to the infinite and unique ways human suffering can manifest, and I am so honored to assist others on their journey of healing. I often feel a deep intuitive understanding of others and the unique conflicts they are struggling with. There is a joy in helping others find their true self and supporting them as they integrate love, freedom, and wellness in their lives. It is so powerful to break the chains of our past, and create a new empowered future, instead of repeating the dysfunctional patterns that imprison us.

In my early days of undergraduate school, I was very drawn to becoming a teacher and had always loved children. During that time, I worked in the Down Syndrome unit at a state hospital, working with toddlers. Every time I walked in there, there were little tiny arms that reached up from a big playpen, each baby asking to be held. They were precious, sweet, and loved to cuddle. These children touched my heart and fostered my wish to help those in need.

During this time, I was also drawn to reading books on yoga, psychology, spirituality, health, and nutrition. The books on yoga and spiritual awareness, always spoke of honoring the body through eating pure, nutritious foods, and to eat peacefully and quietly. This idea both fascinated and attracted me. After reading one of my first books on nutrition, I felt truly inspired. I remember standing on a chair in my college apartment holding the book, and looking at the list of unhealthy ingredients to avoid, like hydrogenated fats, preservatives, and chemicals I couldn't pronounce. I then began throwing away the cans and boxes that my roommates and I had just bought. When my roommates returned, they asked me what I had done with all the food? Needless to say, they were not appreciative.

Soon, I became fascinated with how to make the things we liked from scratch with healthy ingredients, instead of all the chemicals inherent in the processed foods we normally ate. I recall being out at a dinner with my family and other guests, where "very special food" was pre-ordered for the party. I realized that I did not want to eat what everyone else was eating, and quietly ordered something else from the menu. My father became very upset with me, because I was being different, and not conforming to what everyone else was eating. He very unhappily looked at me, and said sighing, "How did the apple fall so far from the tree?" I felt hurt by his comment, however it wouldn't change my resolve to not eat a meal that I didn't want and felt wasn't right for my body.

Looking back, I realize that this was the beginning of my becoming an independent thinker, and finding a way to exercise my freedom to choose what I did and didn't want for myself. The ability to make that choice has helped me greatly, and has been the foundation of how I have lived my life ever since. Having healthy boundaries with food and other life decisions, and being true to oneself is essential for wellness. Having the inner freedom to make healthy choices for ourselves, no matter where we are, or whom we are with, and having the respect to not judge others, is personally empowering.

I then spent many years studying, experimenting, and learning about health. I went the Hippocrates Health Institute in West Palm Beach, Florida, which was an eye-opening education about plant-based and raw foods, detoxification, healing our bodies, and staying well. What I learned there became part of me, and I continued to build knowledge of healing foods from plant-based sources. This led me to eventually become a nutritionist and a functional medicine practitioner. Functional medicine looks at the whole person and the underlying causes of conditions, rather than treat only the symptoms. I am so grateful for finding this path, and I feel strongly that this evolution could only have happened because I first had the wish, and then commitment, to be well, and was willing to work through my own struggles, conflicts, and difficulties. Looking back, that self-work was indeed the deepest training and preparation one can have in order to help others on their journey. I deeply feel that to be vital throughout our lives is to be in a state of inspiration and creativity, and to have a willingness to grow and learn from the challenges set before us.

As I longed for new insights and understandings about myself and about life, I became enthralled with mentors and teachers that seemed kind and wise. As we all know, there are some teachings that are, by their very nature, very uncomfortable; they push our buttons and touch places in us where all our resistances and pain hide away. When these discomforts occur, it often does not seem like a teaching at the time, however, when we look back in hindsight, we become aware of the lessons we learned from our challenges.

I loved reading books about the evolution of the path of spiritual masters, and was deeply affected reading Hermann Hesse's *Siddhartha*, *The Autobiography of a Yogi* by Paramahansa Yogananda, and *Be Here Now* by Ram Dass. As a seeker at the beginning of my journey, I was open to and praying for special teachers to come into my life. I was invited to a gathering one evening, to see a performance of a man called The Singing Rabbi. I was sitting in a room with about 200 people waiting for the performance to begin, and in walked Shlomo Carlebach. Before he entered the stage, he greeted each and everyone individually in the room, with warm, loving eyes and a welcoming heart. I was amazed by this, never having seen anyone do anything like this before. He then went on stage with his guitar and began teaching in this very soulful way. He was a wonderful storyteller, and the stories that he told were expressed in such deeply heartfelt and powerful way. He sang songs, told parables, and sang soul-stirring rhythms that made everyone want to get up off their chairs, hold hands, and dance together in a circle to the spiritual rhythms he created. This was one of the most moving and spiritual experiences of my life.

After this night, a small group of students and I became Shlomo's students. We would gather together, and Shlomo would light a candle and teach us beautiful, moving, and deeply spiritual teachings from the Jewish holy texts. He became my rabbi and my teacher, and I will always feel blessed to have known him.

After graduating with my degree in Early Childhood Education, I began working in a day care in the South Bronx of New York, with precious three-year-old children. Many of the children in my class were living in challenging situations. I loved teaching young children, and I soon enrolled in a masters degree program in Early Childhood Education. As I continued to work with the children and their families, whom I cared deeply for, I began to recognize many serious underlying problems in their lives. A longing started in me to help them in a different way, but this was not fully recognized by me until later on.

At the same time, I had begun studying yoga at the Integral Yoga Institute in NYC. I eventually met Swami Satchidananda from India, the spiritual teacher and founder of the institute, who was a beautiful, shining, wise, and peaceful soul. I began going on silent yoga retreats through the institute, and was amazed by the experience of being silent. I was able to hear the inner noise of my own mind for the first time, and I was doing yoga and meditation practices all day, including karma yoga, which was a period of giving service. Karma Yoga was an amazing experience. Each time there was a retreat, the yogis in charge of running the retreat would go to the facility's owners and inquire about what physical improvements were needed in that particular facility, and the group of us would work in teams, in silence, to help. It was love and service in action. Swami Satchidananda taught us to always leave a place nicer than it was before you got there. This was an early and inspiring teaching for me about giving back and offering compassionate help. I remember that one of my tasks was to clean statues in a beautiful chapel in Mt. Holyoke Monastery where the retreat was being held. I learned so much from Swami Satchidananda.

He was so joyful and loved to laugh, and was one of my deepest spiritual teachers.

Soon after, I was invited to meet, Ruth, a friend's mother. She had become a disciple of Master Kirpal Singh. I heard Ruth's amazing stories of his powerful spirituality, and attended their group meditations. I was then blessed to be invited to NYC to be part of a private satsang with Kirpal Singh and Ruth's family. I remember walking into the room where he was sitting. He looked huge and powerful to me, with beautiful, piercing light coming out of his eyes and flowing toward all of us in the room. I felt a very powerful spiritual energy, which has always stayed with me from that day. It touched my soul, and awakened something in me that I now realize has always been growing within. I was blessed to receive this beautiful gift, which has been an important catalyst in my spiritual growth. As all these experiences were going on in my life, I was also powerfully drawn to psychological healing and therapy. As I was looking for my spiritual teachers, I was also looking for my therapist.

In my graduate school program, I began to notice the extensive crossover of education and psychology, and I was now taking many courses in psychology to fulfill my credits and requirements. One of the classes I took was a course in humanistic psychology, and my professor was a Gestalt therapist. He invited me to attend a Gestalt therapy workshop at his office, and I was excited and intrigued to attend. The workshop was interactive and experiential. During one exercise, we had to walk around the room and pick someone to share with. I was drawn to a wonderful woman whose name is Reggie. We were supposed to share what work we did. I shared that I was an early childhood teacher, finishing my masters, and I loved what I did. Reggie shared with me that she was a psychologist with a masters degree in psychology. In that moment, I felt a shock go through me. I was immediately drawn to the realization of how much I wanted to become a psychotherapist. Until that moment, I had been on the track to be a teacher, and never questioned that I should be doing something different. All of a sudden, my purpose in life crystallized in that exchange with Reggie. I thought I was done with school, which was evidently not the case.

Soon after I finished my education program, I began my Masters in Clinical Mental Health Counseling. This was a defining moment for me, as I was beginning my studies to become a psychotherapist. As I look back, I realize that so much came together for me at that moment of recognition; my early attraction to therapy, when I knew nothing about it, and then the magnificent epiphany that this is what I had really wanted to do all along.

During this time, I came across the writings of one of my heroes, Dr. Viktor Frankl, a young Austrian Psychiatrist during World War II, who was inspired to open his practice soon after graduating school, but was heartbreakingly captured and imprisoned in a concentration camp. He had been writing a manuscript on his insights into human psychology, and the Nazis took it away and destroyed it. His invincible spirit led him to continue with his book, and so Dr. Frankl began again, writing on little scraps of paper, which he hid in the hem of his clothes. He had many further realizations during his imprisonment having to do with the human spirit overcoming adversity.

It was after he was released from the camp, that he wrote his seminal work, *Man's Search for Meaning,* published in 1946. From this work came one of his best-known quotes, "The one thing you can't take away from me is the way I choose to respond to what you do to me. The last of one's freedoms is to choose one's attitude in any given circumstance." [1]

Freedom is being empowered to live the life you want, reflected in your choices, actions, integrity, self respect, and in how you honor others. Viktor Frankl coined the term, "positive defiance," which is to defy the

---

[1]Frankl, Viktor. *Man's Search for Meaning.* Beacon Press: Boston, 1946.

negative and move towards the positive.[2] By challenging yourself to do something positive, you create positive chemicals in your brain. It might sound like a paradox, but empowered choice of how we will respond is freedom.

Often, the events that occur in life are so intensely uncomfortable and painful, but in finding our freedom, and the wisdom to react in the most constructive way possible, we can embark on a journey of self-growth. Life has so much possible joy, and it also has so much loss and heartbreak, and we are challenged to embrace it all. In my experience, the more we are open to the synchronicities of life, the more amazing connections show up in our lives. It's as if there is a team upstairs working on our "case" and they arrange these seemingly coincidental circumstances that even the most creative writer could never have thought of. I often think that truth is stranger than fiction, and that there is much more going on behind the scenes than the seeming coincidences of life. We come to realize that the world we live in is messy and often bittersweet, with a plentiful combination of blessings and hardships that push us to our limits. We are forced to deal with things we never thought of, and grow in ways we did not realize we would.

As I began my Masters in Clinical Mental Health Counseling, one of the requirements for students was to enter therapy ourselves. I had been looking for the right therapist for me for a number of years, and it was during this time that I finally found him; he said powerful things to me that helped me from the very first session. I worked very hard, and for a very long time, in this psychoanalytic psychotherapy treatment. I treasure what I learned from those sessions, and how this therapy helped me become who I truly was. It also was the most excellent training for my burgeoning profession as a psychotherapist. I feel that it is crucial for every psychotherapist to work deeply and profoundly on themselves to be

---

[2]Frankl, Viktor. *Man's Search for Meaning*. Beacon Press: Boston, 1946.

able to do very deep work with others. You cannot take others where you yourself aren't willing to go, and I have to say at this point, that none of us are without wounds that need attention and healing.

I also spent many years in professional training, group psychotherapy, and group and individual supervision, which helped me develop in my work as a psychotherapist. During this time, I was doing an internship and working for an orthomolecular psychiatrist, who was working with psychiatry and nutrition. I remember meeting an excellent nutritionist, at the center where I was working, who was about to leave the center, just as I was beginning there. She once told me something that has since played an integral part in my philosophy, "There is no stress we cannot handle if we are well nourished." I will always remember this piece of wisdom. It planted a seed in me that has grown within ever since.

Also making a powerful impression on me during that time, was working with alcoholics who were physically and emotionally ravaged by their disease. They were being given psychotherapy, addiction treatment, and nutrition intervention, which had a powerful impact on them. Nutritional intervention was rarely included in treatment for alcoholism at that time, though it is significant to the healing process. I saw significant improvements in these people by their receiving this comprehensive approach. I couldn't have known by this point that this was foreshadowing for my future work.

Years later, I met another wise nutritionist, who I became close with through referring patients to each other, and had many discussions about our mutual love of nutrition. She was getting ready to retire, and was interviewing nutritionists with the purpose of finding the right person to take over her practice. Ironically, she and I had very similar nutritional and spiritual philosophies, and I had been attending ongoing workshops and lectures about nutrition. I was fascinated and drawn to the mind-body connection, and how psychology and nutrition worked together.

One day, my nutritionist friend said to me, "I would like you to take over my practice," I smiled, greatly appreciating the thought. I responded that I would love to, but I already had a practice that I love, and I didn't have a degree in nutrition. She told me to go back to school! I remember feeling very nervous and excited at the thought of actually studying nutrition in school. Shortly after, I enrolled in school, and two years later, I became a Certified Nutritionist. I then had the challenge of becoming a practitioner in nutrition and integrating it into my psychotherapy practice. I feel this was one of the very best decisions I made in my entire life.

As I integrated nutrition and psychology together, I learned so much more about wellness, and am so grateful for now having a bigger toolbox for helping people; the powerful and essential mind-body connection affects every health issue, whether it originates in psychology or in nutrition.

I then completed training in functional medicine, and a fellowship in anti-aging medicine. I truly believe in lifelong learning. Every teacher I met, led to much more reading and exploration of additional therapeutic and spiritual teachings. These then led to a commitment to ongoing growth that will always be such an important part of my life.

As my integrative practice took off, one question continued to pop up over and over again: "Why, with all the knowledge and wisdom out there today, are so many people still struggling and suffering?" It seems that there is often a huge chasm between what we know intellectually, what we are working towards emotionally, and our ability to follow through with actions that honor ourselves, and our goals. I wanted to figure out why it is so hard for us to integrate what we know, with what we actually do.

It is very important to know that these difficult issues can be healed with an integrative approach of psychotherapy, nutritional and lifestyle changes, spiritual principles, and other modalities if needed. It is something I try to practice in my, and my family's, everyday life, and it has, without a doubt, changed our lives for the better.

The Psychology of Wellness

Chapter Three

If you really want to do something, you'll find a way.
If you don't, you'll find an excuse."
—Jim Rohn

When I think of the true meaning of the psychology of wellness, I think of the opportunity for hope and the possibility for positive change in our lives. As a practitioner, my mission is to help support patients to become more whole and integrated in light of all the human challenges that life can bring. I support them in becoming more connected to themselves, and more empowered to make positive changes in their lives. While the symphony of all the challenges that human beings face rages on, we still need to attend to our health and wellness needs. It is an interconnected process. Just as when inflammation starts in the body it goes everywhere, so does healing spread throughout. No matter where you start this process, as you improve your wellness, new healing and inspiration will begin to flow to every part of you.

As mentioned earlier, in my opinion, there is more psychology in nutrition than nutrition. As a long time health practitioner, I have learned that we all have something to heal. Many people have a longing to bring more wellness into their lives, and often hear the word "wellness" echoing in the background of their mind, as well in the media. Even though they desire to make changes, they often need support, education, and therapy to truly be able to implement these changes. In addition to the individualized nutritional programs that I provide, many people need nutritional psychotherapy to truly change their relationship with their body, and to implement good self-care. I've seen many people who've found nutritional programs prior to coming to me that they were not able to follow, because the essential psychological part of changing was never addressed.

It is important to remember that this is a human problem, and that you are not alone. There seems to be an epidemic of stress and disconnection in many people. We know we want to do better for ourselves, but often, the choices we make are in conflict with this goal. Why is that? How we eat is so psychologically complex; it is truly a reflection of how we feel about and treat ourselves. Why does one person at an office go through the fast food drive-through during their break, and another brings a healthy lunch from home, made with care? By looking at why we make these decisions, or develop these habits, it helps us to face our challenges, so we can set the stage for a new foundation of wellness in ourselves.

Wellness is not just about how we eat. It is about the functioning of our psychology in its entirety, and the hidden wounds that need healing and support. We must eat food for biological sustenance; it is the primary reason we need to eat. However, in the arena of complex human psychology, we find that we also use food for other purposes. We use food as a social activity, and as a device for calming and soothing discomfort, a sort of drug to alter our moods of loneliness, anger, boredom, and frustration. People habitually numb themselves with comfort food, not knowing how to constructively process the uncomfortable feelings of stress or worry that they may be feeling. This misuse of food is a great distraction from the essential, and powerfully life changing actions that we really need to focus on. This harmful patterning really decimates our self-esteem, but many people live in this kind of fog indefinitely. They are in a state of emotional numbness, unaware of the damage they are doing to themselves.

We carry deep within us family imprints of food memories that have great impact on us. These memories, in turn, influence our thinking processes, our longings for unhealthy foods, and our choices. It is only when people begin to wake up and create the changes that can set them free in the long run, instead of choosing impulsive actions that they continually regret, that real healing can take place. By making these deep-seated memories and wounds more conscious, we can know what is influencing us, and then make more empowered choices based on that greater awareness.

Creating healthy boundaries is essential. How many of you have been confronted with the pressure of what others want us to eat, and risk getting them upset if we choose not to eat particular foods anymore, or join in on their food escapades? We have social demands of what others expect from us in terms of sharing food experiences. By changing our way of eating altogether, it can be very upsetting to others around us who are invested in keeping us in line with their own patterns and habits. They are threatened by a fear of change, of deprivation, or even judgment. How you set your boundaries determines the level at which you can fill your own needs, when it comes to your own health and wellbeing. What are your boundaries? If you struggle with upholding your boundaries, what is the fear that shows up when you hold strong to your boundaries?

Fear that others won't like or love you
Fear that others won't approve of you
Fear of your own power
Fear of success
Fear of change

These fears keep us from taking care of ourselves. We often tend to rationalize and display other resistances when it comes to eating and lifestyle changes. What is fear, anyway? I always like to use the acronym definition:

F= False

E= Evidence

A= Appearing

R= Real

This is a helpful reminder that a lot of what we fear is from our own inner projections and imagination. Fearful thoughts are how we scare ourselves.

Thought always precedes behaviors, even if we are unaware of those preceding thoughts. When someone says to me that they found themselves eating something damaging without any memory of choosing to eat, I often ask them, "What did you say to yourself right before you did this?" You'd be surprised by the answers. Or maybe, some of you reading this wouldn't be...

I see so many people who are continually suffering from the mistaken and destructive decisions that they have made, continually dealing with ongoing fallout and misery from those decisions. The only thing we can do when that is the case is, take full responsibility, own the pain that your actions caused you and the others involved, have true remorse, work on yourself to heal and do whatever you can to make amends for your actions. One of the most painful things is when someone has hurt others and they do not want to truly face the pain they caused they prevent the healing that can be possible. What I am saying is not easy, but deeply worth it in the long run of one's life. Learning how to use good judgment, in all aspects of our lives, saves those that depend on us.

But what ultimately keeps us from taking the plunge and doing the hard and rewarding work of taking care of ourselves? Maybe you recognize some of these rationalizations:

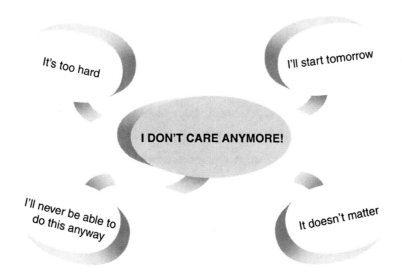

It's too hard

I'll start tomorrow

I DON'T CARE ANYMORE!

I'll never be able to do this anyway

It doesn't matter

These rationalizations, in turn, lead to self-destructive behaviors:

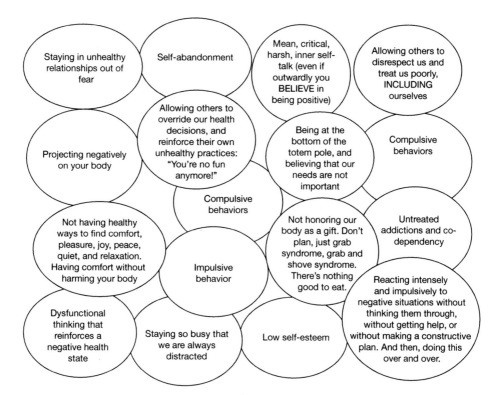

Staying in unhealthy relationships out of fear

Self-abandonment

Mean, critical, harsh, inner self-talk (even if outwardly you BELIEVE in being positive)

Allowing others to disrespect us and treat us poorly, INCLUDING ourselves

Allowing others to override our health decisions, and reinforce their own unhealthy practices: "You're no fun anymore!"

Being at the bottom of the totem pole, and believing that our needs are not important

Compulsive behaviors

Projecting negatively on your body

Compulsive behaviors

Not having healthy ways to find comfort, pleasure, joy, peace, quiet, and relaxation. Having comfort without harming your body

Impulsive behavior

Not honoring our body as a gift. Don't plan, just grab syndrome, grab and shove syndrome. There's nothing good to eat.

Untreated addictions and co-dependency

Dysfunctional thinking that reinforces a negative health state

Staying so busy that we are always distracted

Low self-esteem

Reacting intensely and impulsively to negative situations without thinking them through, without getting help, or without making a constructive plan. And then, doing this over and over.

Destructive thinking like this leads to "stuckness," and a cycle of impulsive action leading to regret, remorse, and self-recrimination. Often, then follows the next declaration, "Now I am going on (the new diet of the moment)...starting tomorrow." Now that new diet is not necessarily sustainable, which then leads us back to the cycle we so deeply want to stop, but don't seem able to. When this process begins to happen within us, that is the time that we need support and healing in order to change our health habits and behaviors. Making the choice to truly change, creates a much greater freedom, and prevents suffering now and in the future.

A beautiful example of this power to change is Mel Zuckerman, the founder of Canyon Ranch, a destination resort spa devoted to wellness. He had had multiple health and weight problems all of his life, and at fifty years old he decided that he had had enough. He began to make lifelong changes in how he approached food, exercise, and emotional and spiritual health. Now, at eighty-five years old, Mel works out every day and is in much better health than when he was in his earlier years. He is a true inspiration and an honor to know; a true example of the precept that what we believe has a huge effect on our health and life. My own experiences have told me that our body, mind, and spirit want to heal in every way possible.

Many years ago, a young woman came to see me who was well over three hundred pounds. She was beautiful, smart, and struggling. She had convinced herself that it was not possible for her to make the profound changes she so desperately needed; she needed deep healing from numerous traumas that had occurred in her life. We worked very deeply and consistently, working on one layer at a time, one step at a time. Now, fifteen years later, she has successfully kept off 150 lbs.! She was amazed that it was possible, yet she had never believed it to be so before. She now has a new vision of herself and is still healing into that. The new confidence and freedom to become who she truly was opened many doors for her, and brought a new career that inspires her every day. She found her true self, her meaning, and purpose, which are essential for everyone's wholeness and wellness. Food and eating had taken on whole new meanings, as she regained respect and love for herself. She took all processed foods, sugar, fast food, and deep-fried food out of her diet. To her surprise, and to many people that I have treated, when these foods are eliminated, we lose our desire for them; our cravings disappear, and our energy, sleep, and digestion improve. Even more surprising, our taste buds change right along with us. Numerous times there will be even be an improvement in mood, memory, and cognition. Brain fog goes away. Our entire being improves, which opens the inspirational door to many more changes in our life. We gain confidence in ourselves that we can do this. And, on a more technical level, but just as exciting, blood tests improve, along with blood pressure and blood sugar. We'll discuss more on the biological part of this process in the next chapter.

So What's at the Core of our Resistance?

Our early experiences construct a theme that often plays out through our lives, and creates our self-image; including how we feed ourselves, our attitude towards our body image, and our health. These primal experiences often form the core perspective of who we think we are. Looking at these perspectives, and where they first began, is crucial in the process of understanding and healing the relationship with our selves.

What was the emotional climate of your family at the time of your birth, when you came to be? This question is important because parents' feelings get transferred into a child's being, pre-verbally. From our earliest beginnings, to when we're speaking in sentences, a child experiences many feelings without having words to express them. Feelings from this pre-verbal time affect and color our feelings towards our self and our view of life.

When a baby is born, we start out by crying, "Waaaaaaa!" We need warmth, love, and safety. We need to be held, to be fed, to connect, and to be able to count on the consistency of our caregiver. When a child is hungry, if their need is responded to with loving care, it conveys a message that their needs are important and that they will be fed when they need it. The rhythm that gets established based on the child's body's need is very significant in terms of inner security. Often, even well meaning mothers are not taught this information and they try to feed their babies on an imposed schedule, rather than when the baby is truly hungry. There is a relationship between this rhythm and a child's emotional development. This is where self-esteem originates, and the defining of who we think we are. Children often feel guilty for needing something that is not being offered, as if they are asking for too much. When, ironically, what they are asking for is totally natural.

Being only human, mothers and fathers can often be in times of crisis of their own, and are not always able to be in tune to fully understand their baby's needs. Divorce, depression, job loss, finances, illness, and other life changes can make a mother or father more stressed, which can impact his or her ability to consistently meet their baby's needs.

Human beings have a deep profound yearning for connection and to be understood. This is a very sensitive area because we feel these needs so deeply, and often because of life circumstances and the challenges we are presented with, some of them are not met. No human being has had a perfect childhood and no one has had every need met, so we become faced with the challenge of those unmet needs and figuring out what to do with them. This often manifests as a feeling of emptiness deep inside that can be unnerving and uncomfortable, and which can lead to the need to fill that void with behaviors that are destructive to us. While we can understand what we are doing to ourselves in the long run, in the short term, the desperate attempt is made to create immediate relief.

At the root of many people's suffering is the feeling of unworthiness. We need to heal this at the core, because this feeling influences so much of our treatment of ourselves. Someone could be very successful, intelligent, kind, and caring, but have deep within them a gnawing feeling that they are not worthy and they do not know why. This is something they cannot rationalize away or come to grips with intellectually. It has to do with healing in the core of our being. A false belief was generated long ago that needs healing and transformation. This feeling of unworthiness contributes to fear, insecurity, and a lack of faith in ourselves. Many people, more than we realize, are quietly suffering in this way. We seek reassurance and safety while these disempowering feelings permeate our best of intentions. One major theme we grapple with is that we are missing a connection with our true self. That is the place of intuition, wisdom, and great potential that we often don't realize we have. This process is about finding that place, connecting to it, integrating it, and living from it.

Many patients have told me that when they were children, they were viewed as being overweight and were told that they needed to be on a diet. This message was often received as a harsh criticism of who they were as a person. They were put on various diets and weight loss programs, and taken to numerous diet doctors. Many people then began to view themselves in this false way and started to direct hate and criticism toward themselves and towards their body; this then exacerbated the problem. These are often the people who had secret stashes of food stuck in their pajama drawer, or under the bed. Ironically, when these same people look back at pictures of themselves from that time, they see that they weren't, in fact, as overweight as they had believed. They had come to believe as children that something was wrong with them, rather than that they had a human challenge that needed to be healed. This is a clear example of a child in conflict, trying to meet their own needs and comfort themselves in the only way they know how, but in direct conflict to the rigid eating plan set in front of them. This leaves the child caught in the vicious cycle of parent approval or disapproval, based on how they eat and their present weight. This is where unworthiness begins. The child often feels good or bad based on whether they are complying with, or resisting, the plan. Many of my adult patients begin their session with me by saying, "I was bad or good this week." Defining one's identity based on being good or bad about their eating is called "toxic shame," referred to by John Bradshaw in his book, *Healing the Shame that Binds You.*[3] My understanding of toxic shame is that when we have a difficulty or have fallen into destructive behavior, we look at ourselves in our totality as defective; we need to, instead, see ourselves as a human being who is worthy, but has a problem and needs help. Here lies the intersection of psychology and nutrition.

Many families have very unhealthy eating patterns, so it may seem normal to them that this is the way people should eat; numerous family members who may have their own struggles with health and weight further complicate this. Food can become the entertainment, the main activity, and the focal point of the family, instead of truly connecting with each other through communication and other meaningful activity. This dysfunctional system is pervasive, and in our memory banks we associate those eating patterns with our family and our communities.

A very typical issue that most children face is the desperate need to

---

[3]Bradshaw, John. *Healing the Shame that Binds* You. Deerfield Beach, FL: HCI, 2005.

fit in and not feel different. If you eat differently, then you can be seen, or treated, as odd and feel as if you are on the outside looking in at "regular" kids. Our attitude toward this makes all the difference in the world, as we can either feel alienated or empowered by our own view of how we are different. Without realizing it, we get very attached both chemically and psychologically to these patterns, although it is possible to break the chain and live your own empowered life.

Many people see eating healthy as a form of deprivation from junk food and foods they're attached to, instead of seeing it as a way to care for and nurture their body. The irony of this is that caring for your body and eating healthy can be greatly pleasurable and satisfying. Expressions of love and support can also be greatly confused with indulging in unhealthy foods that have numerous destructive qualities. When a child gets an "A" on his or her report card, are they rewarded with ice cream? If a class succeeds at a group goal, are they given a pizza or donut party? What happens when parents request healthy choices for their children, and then the grandparents in charge of their children for the day, take them to a fast food restaurant to indulge them? What's of greatest concern is developing an ingrained pattern of food used as rewards, or as special treats for any accomplishments. This is the beginning of misinformed self-care; how we give to ourselves when we deserve a treat, as we get older.

In recognition of this problem at a school level, nowadays many school districts have begun to implement a "no food as reward" policy, and though only healthy food choices are allowed in the classroom, the practice is still pervasive. However, this issue becomes much more complicated at the family level. There are many different people in a child's life that will attempt to indulge them with junk food. In our society, we are inundated with food from so many directions and for so many different reasons, and that stimulates overeating. As a result, many people lose touch with their real hunger and fullness, and disconnect from their body's signals to stop eating. There is a bio-chemical component, an addiction to processed and refined foods, which, when combined with the emotional component, really plays havoc with our attempt to self-regulate our eating. If a child develops the pattern that food is a reward, then they most likely become an adult who sees food as a reward.

That brings us to the need to break these chains of the past. Perhaps you are now challenged by a health issue of the body, mind, or spirit, or by a deep longing for a profound change in your life. Maybe you feel it's time to start paying attention to your lifestyle and your eating. This is the beginning of self-love; the realization that you have not been treating yourself with love, and even though it's an intellectually attractive concept, you don't know how to actualize it in your behavior. Realizing that the lack of self-love comes from the experiences in your past that have created your beliefs about yourself, is the first step in the journey toward love and a deep acceptance of who you are. And to support this, you need an empowered approach that assists you in raising your self-esteem, self-respect, and self-honor, and enables you to take better care of yourself.

Endless Search, Vicious Cycle

The vicious cycle is a universal problem and a human struggle that numerous people from every walk of life, every background, and every level of education struggle with.

Paradox Box:

I know what to do, but I can't get myself to do it.

This is something that has been said to me many hundreds of times, and often is said as an assumption of where people are and how they've gotten stuck there, rather than what's actually true. There develops a kind of mental block when it comes to incorporating healthy changes into action; a sense of not cooperating with oneself, one's dreams and desires, to realize a certain goal in terms of their health and weight. Even if they want to make the change, and they dream about making the change, until they take the actions required, the change remains a dream. Sometimes it requires building a new inner structure to be able to live in this new way.

So let's talk about where we get stuck. If you were to take an honest inventory of where you get stuck, where are the places where that would be?

Try this little quiz, and be honest with yourself:

- ✓ Where are you stuck?
- ✓ Do you not know where to begin?
- ✓ Do you believe it's possible to get there?
- ✓ Are you open to change?
- ✓ Do you give up easily?
- ✓ What do you believe about your stuckness?

Take a look at your answers and begin to observe how your mind plays into sabotaging you from what you truly want. The mind is fertile with ways to talk us out of those things that we most want. Often people don't realize that they have made a conscious or unconscious decision to play out self-sabotaging eating behaviors. It often feels like an impulsive act that they hadn't thought about at all. They were going a hundred miles an hour in their head, did the behavior, and then started to feel the negative consequences. This is followed by remorse and anger at themselves. What I know to be true is that any action we take is preceded by a thought and a decision, no matter how fast it goes across our mental screen. We are making a decision to either act on this thought or to set a healthy boundary. Telling the truth to our self is the first step to healing and changing, and the beginning of believing that change is possible.

Let's take a look at the vicious cycle we often find ourselves trapped in. Does this sound familiar to you? Something occurs in your world that triggers a negative emotional feeling state like fear, anxiety, boredom, emptiness, loneliness, or anger, which then brings about a projection of negative thoughts about the outcome of that circumstance. Not knowing how to comfort and soothe ourselves in a constructive way, we fall into a pattern of going to food as a mood-altering drug to numb us from our discomfort and to give us a momentary relief from our pain. We will rationalize, con, manipulate ourselves, and others if necessary, debate, argue, fight with ourselves in our head, and then act on the impulse to eat in a destructive way. In this vicious cycle, our emotional response tells us to turn to food. We turn against ourselves, and our desire for our own good health, wellness, and healthy ideal weight, when we use food as medication.

Then we enter the "Why did I do this?" stage. We start to feel sad, remorseful, regretful, guilty, and disappointed. We have emotional and

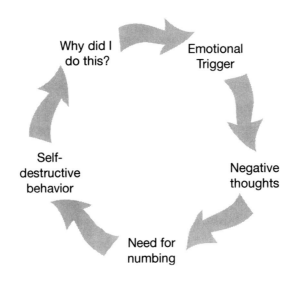

physical reactions. The scale goes up, we feel bloated, more uncomfortable, tired, and sick. Emotionally, we become angry with ourselves, and beat ourselves into submission for having fallen from grace. We begin looking again for a new solution, such as a punishing, restrictive diet or exercise regimen. It is not long before we begin to feel bored, deprived, and miserable on this new routine. We eventually mount a rebellion in reaction to this restrictive or punishing diet, and go back into battle with ourselves when we see our plan didn't work. This creates a newly triggered negative emotive reaction and we are back at the beginning of this vicious cycle again. We are destined to go round and round, until we finally learn how to break the cycle, and begin to truly know how to take care of ourselves once and for all. It's like going on a journey into the forest to find gold, then losing your way and falling into a ditch over and over again. What is the teaching in that for us? Why do we keep falling into the ditch? Wouldn't we want to create a better path?

Self-Criticism and Personal Suffering

We often base our approval of ourselves and our lovability on our appearance, weight, and perceived overall wellness. That perception is destructive and severely limiting to our vision of who we truly are as a full person. Being self-critical and hurtful because we have a difficulty, is not real love; it is a dysfunctional, conditional version of love. We use that perception to define our identity, rather than acknowledging that each of these things is only one aspect of who we are. In this dysfunction, we will trick ourselves into never finding peace and never finding an answer... because there is no answer. We're left feeling hopeless, and wondering why we can do so many other things well, why not this? *That* is personal suffering. It doesn't matter what degrees you have or how intelligent you are, this suffering can't be resolved by an intellectual "to do" list; it can't be fixed in the same way as a corporate merger or a surgical procedure. The answer lies much deeper within.

We have this inner, harshly critical voice that beats us up and contributes to our confusion and inability to stick to the plan. It may show up as, "I'm a loser," "Nothing works for me," "I can't change," and "I don't deserve anything good." These inner messages convince us that any attempt to better ourselves is futile. This act of self-humiliation further erodes our sense of self. Our circular unexplored thinking creates destructive negative beliefs about ourselves, which we treat as the gospel because it came out of our own head. It could be the worst possible advice for us, but we practice it over and over again anyway. The inner arguing and defeating self-talk cause us to throw in the towel and give up. By taking the frustration and hurt out on our self, we continually sabotage our original good intentions.

If you don't already have the foundation of seeing yourself as a whole being that is worthy of love, support, and kindness, then creating that is the necessary first step of the process. Instead of watching the same show over and over, change the channel within, and create a new way of relating to your body and your self.

Functional and Dysfunctional Relationships

Functional relationships

Functional relationships are a powerful foundation for long-term, intimate, and emotionally safe connections with others. When relationships are functional, they exemplify honor and respect for the dignity of both people involved. Both people have each other's best interest in mind, and live it in their actions. It involves both self-development work and couple processing, in order to work toward having a functional relationship. It is both a privilege and a responsibility to be authentic and to be supported for being who you truly are. Functional relationships create stability, goodness, and a foundation for ongoing, deepening love.

Some qualities of functional relationships are:
- Love and appreciation of who each other is
- Mutual respect
- Empathy, compassion, and a desire to understand each other
- Communicate constructively
- High integrity
- Loyalty to each other
- Supportive and connected to each other even when you are not together
- Focus sexual energy on partner, which creates safety, trust, and emotional intimacy
- Both people are thoughtful, considerate, and caring
- Face adversity together, helping each other to grow
- Are capable of deeply and sincerely apologizing, with remorse and humility
- Are able to face, resolve, and work through problems together, constructively and respectfully
- Both people are willing to work on the relationship, and build an ongoing, stronger foundation of trust, respect, and self-responsibility
- Understand and deeply care about what makes the other feel loved and respected, and express this in each other's actions
- Respect the individuality of each other, with their wishes, dreams, and aspirations.
- Help and support each other in reaching their potential
- Realizing that every relationship is a work in progress, and needs to be treated with love and care

Dysfunctional relationships

I have seen the toll that chronic toxic relationships take on a person's body, mind, and spirit. They wear you down, and ravage your spirit. Facing whether or not you are in a dysfunctional relationship, can lead to saving your health and, ultimately, your life. Getting the true help you need is available. Reach out for it, be brave, and become the hero in your own life. Transformation is possibly by taking the time to work on yourself to understand your psychology, how your psychology fits with your partner's psychology, and what needs to change in you, even if your partner is not open to changing. Examining what new healthy boundaries you need for yourself, and incorporating them into your being, will be the beginning of positive changes in your life. Often people do not believe something hopeful is possible if they can't imagine it.

Some qualities present in dysfunctional relationships:
- Self-centeredness
- A demanding and ungrateful attitude
- Excessive anger, negativity, and put downs
- Lying
- Cheating
- Lack of empathy and compassion
- Fighting destructively, and saying horribly cruel words that create scars
- Resentment continually building up from unresolved problems. They add to the stack of arguments that are over, but not fully healed, and people gradually become numb to each other.
- Verbal or physical abuse
- Disrespect
- Feeling afraid of your partner and what they might do
- Unpredictable moods and behavior
- Embarrassing you in a certain way, even when you've asked them not to
- Untreated addictions, and refusing to get help and recovery

- Refusing to get therapy to help a relationship in trouble
- Children being hurt by witnessing this relationship, which affects them on a deep level
- Children hearing mean fights between the parents that they love, and feeling torn apart
- Co-dependency (See section below)
- A lack of understanding of your or your partner's needs, their emotional pain, or their loneliness
- Insensitive to others' deeper needs and feelings
- Argues, is defensive, puts up walls, and is unreachable emotionally
- Doesn't keep their word, and is not dependable
- Blames other for all their problems
- One partner judges the other for not getting over a past hurt that they imposed on them, just because time has gone by. The other partner feels ongoing hurts that have not been healed or understood.
- Not taking responsibility for one's behavior and actions, and the effect it has on the other person
- Inappropriate, insensitive sexual behavior that upsets the other

Finding a healthy partner and relationship

Many people long to find a healthy relationship, but are often confused and unsure how to proceed in a constructive way. They are conflicted about how and where to find a healthy partner, what qualities are most important to look for, and what are the biggest red flags to recognize as soon as possible. People of all ages ask for help in this area. By establishing healthy boundaries for yourself, you will prevent much suffering when meeting a potential new partner. Picking a healthy partner, begins with inner self work. The more we see in, the more we see out.

The most important qualities to look for when dating:
- Excellent character
- Respectful
- Keeps their word from the beginning
- Does not abuse substances or have addictive behaviors
- Is single and ready to create a meaningful relationship
- Insightful and introspective
- Has a good sense of humor
- Has the ability to listen and be present emotionally
- Hears the importance of what is vulnerably shared and gradually revealed by each person, with earned trust
- Hardworking, respectful, loyal, and high integrity
- Is respectful and responsible with money
- Open to self-growth
- Considers effective communication to be essential

What are the most important red flags to run from?
- The person you meet says that they want a relationship, and may even put themselves out on dating websites, but when it actually comes down to it, they are confused and not sure they are ready. Confusing mixed messages often signal physical or emotional unavailability.
- They say inappropriate things that bother you, often from the very first conversation. For example, maybe they make sexual comments, without even really knowing you. Is that all they can think of talking about? What does this say about their psyche, or intentions?
- They have poor boundaries, and they tell you too much or too little, too soon.
- They only talk about themselves, without asking about you or really listen to you when you speak.

- They display signs of addictive behavior, which they minimize and dismiss.
- Drinks, or uses drugs, and drives
- Wants to go 100 miles an hour in relationship, instead of gradually getting to know each other. It takes time to get to know someone, and their deeper self, even if you are crazy about them.
- Gives you a bad or uncomfortable feeling. Explore this within yourself, and do not ignore it. It could be an intuitive red flag, even if you can't put your finger on what's wrong yet. Trust yourself if you feel unsafe.

Co-Dependency

Co-dependent people are controlled by the belief that, "I can't like me, unless you like me." They are lacking a sense of their own true self, which is what they need to be able to truly take care of themselves, and they tend to have low self-esteem and poor boundaries. People who are co-dependent can be more vulnerable to being taken advantage of, and will often sacrifice their own wellbeing and needs, for another's. They often live in denial of their own difficulties, and their partner's addictions or dysfunction, and often overcompensate for their partner's behavior. Co-dependency can be emotionally painful, and depending on the situation, can totally deplete someone of their healthy life energy. There is much available therapy and treatment for healing co-dependency, by learning to set healthy boundaries and create positive self-esteem.

Depression and Anxiety

There are people in every walk of life, every culture, and every background who suffer from anxiety and depression, among other mental health difficulties. In my opinion, these symptoms signal the need to look at our whole being, to gain a true understanding and grasp of how and why someone is suffering in this way. Anxiety and depression involve our psychology (our emotional past and present), our neurochemistry, our nutrition, the lifestyle we live, and the beliefs we hold.

For example, let's say that someone has had a difficult family experience as a child, in which there are covered-over wounds that have never healed. Maybe they also eat poorly; eating a highly processed, junk food diet with lots of sugar, caffeine, and chemicals. This person overdrinks alcohol at times, has deficient, poor quality sleep, and has little capacity for self-care. All these criteria can make someone more vulnerable to anxiety, depression, or other chronic mood disorders. How could this person feel well?

There is so much that can be done for someone suffering like this, on numerous levels. But what if they never got the right help? What if no one ever asked them about what they are eating and drinking? What if their attitude toward life, and their underlying unhealed hurt, is never addressed? What will happen to this person? When someone is chronically sad or anxious, having an evaluation and excellent psychotherapy can be deeply helpful. It can add a greater self-understanding, as the underlying causes are made clear. Even in this day and age, many people are afraid of psychotherapy and avoid looking for the help that they need. But there are so many positive possibilities available today; there are numerous holistic approaches to healing anxiety and depression. Psychotherapy, nutrition therapy, empowerment, and empathetic understanding are essential in the process of resolving, improving, and healing our mental health and wellness.

This brings to mind a recent potent image I saw on television earlier this year. There was a prison reality show on, and the warden had just handed out, to every prisoner, a copy of *Man's Search for Meaning* by Dr. Viktor Frankl! I was so touched by the positive tool the warden had given to the men. By giving out this very special, possibly life-changing, book to the prisoners he was overseeing, he gave them the opportunity to understand themselves in a new way. There are so many people in need of emotional healing and support who are not receiving it.

Addictive and Compulsive Behavior

> "I believe that owning our worthiness is the act of acknowledging that we are sacred. Perhaps embracing vulnerability and over coming numbing is ultimately about the care and feeding of our spirit."
> —Brene Brown, *Daring Greatly*

When human beings deal with addiction, it really touches my heart. I have a high level of concern for how serious and far-reaching the problem is in our country and the world. There is so much suffering due to addiction, which affects many lives. There are so many people, children, wives, husbands, and significant others, that are hurting from addiction, either their own or a loved one's whose life deeply affects theirs. Active addiction is like a tsunami with a great power of destruction in its path. There is tremendous denial about addiction; what it actually looks like and its potency.

For example, a young woman goes on a date with a young man she is very interested in and wants to get to know better. Over dinner, they order a glass of wine, and as her date is finishing his glass, she notices that he continuously orders alcoholic drinks. He has five to six drinks during dinner, and plans to have even more later. Her heart sinks as he continues to drink, realizing this cute guy who had seemed so bright, funny, and charming, has a drinking problem. She begins to connect the dots from previous conversations she's had with him, when he made references about getting drunk with his friends. She also recalls the comments other people have made to her about his drinking. After watching his behavior at the dinner table, his pattern became clearer to her and began to raise red flags. What she will do then, depends on her awareness, her self-esteem, and her ability to set healthy boundaries. Is this young woman going to make internal excuses for his behavior with alcohol? Is she going to get in the car with him, even if he says he is fine? Or is she going to say, "I don't think you should be driving now after having so many drinks. I will not drive with you." She might have just saved both of their lives as well as other innocent people as well. Sadly, many people would still get in the car, even though they know they shouldn't, as they are risking their lives.

So why do we do this? Are we afraid to upset the other person? Maybe they will be mad at us, or think we overreacted. (Which is exactly what someone using would think and say.) This is where our own clarity, boundaries, and healthy assertiveness become crucial, and may even determine life and death.

Every day, there are all ages of people drinking destructively, even if they're not driving. If they are drinking and driving, then they are in serious denial. This issue is so alarming and causes such pain and tragedy every single day. The organization MADD (Mothers Against Drunk Driving) and other organizations are always trying to alert people to how many deaths or other accidents or illnesses are alcohol-related. This is true for all substances or destructive behaviors.

Key Points in the Addiction Process

An addict uses a substance to mood alter, or to cope with negative emotions or uncomfortable situations, instead turning to their inner strength and finding constructive solutions to their problems. Part of the recovery process is to create an inner emotional home where our wisdom grows and can help guide us. People in active addiction do not have an inner home, and they do not develop emotionally, so they rely on a substance to keep them numb. They don't know how to be with themselves without using. They continue using or doing a certain addictive behavior even though they are already having terrible outcomes and consequences. They are angry if anyone tries to talk to them about it, and they are in denial of how serious this behavior is, the effects on their life, their relationships on all levels, and most of all, the suffering of those that love them.

One of the greatest gifts to give our loved ones is to go into recovery, when it's needed. This can happen through Alcoholics Anonymous, or the appropriate 12-step meeting, psychotherapy, rehab, and making a deep commitment to becoming responsible, available, and well. One of the greatest examples of love, freedom, and wellness is living in recovery one day at a time. It is crucial to truly gain an understanding of what addiction is, and to seek the resources available for recovery. It takes great courage for one to realize it, face it, and make a commitment to a healing and life-affirming process. I feel it is important to note here, that just by eliminating an addictive substance or behavior without a recovery plan will leave a significant part of the healing process unfinished. They still have the underlying and unresolved issues within, and still act upon them. This is an improvement, but without a significant part of the deeper realization and inner self-growth that is needed. Addiction is about your entire relationship with yourself and your approach to life. In our society, there are many people fearing being lonely and empty. This fear can manifest in addictive behaviors.

In addition to the harder addictions of drugs, alcohol, and eating disorders, many of us have soft addictions to keep ourselves distracted, such as always needing something to watch, read, go shopping, or surfing the internet so we don't have to be alone with ourselves. Some cultures and belief systems actually have a goal to achieve emptiness, so that space can be filled with deep spirituality, and so the deeper truths of life have a chance to come through. The more we fear aloneness, the more we stay away from our true essence, and the more empty we feel, which leads us to turn to behaviors that leave us spiritually bankrupt.

There is an epidemic today with technology, in which many people are constantly looking at multiple screens simultaneously, such as a computer and a cellphone, and are easily bored if they are not being constantly stimulated. It's not just children who fall prey to this compulsive behavior. Adults often have difficulty sitting in silence without a television on, especially if they are home alone, and can even rival teenagers with the obsessive checking of their cellphones and texting. Why are we afraid of being quiet and alone with ourselves?

Eating Addiction

There are various eating disorders, such as Anorexia, Bulimia, Compulsive Eating, and combinations of them, which all have a common denominator. They share a disconnect in one's relationship with their true self, which needs healing and attention. It is amazing what we are capable of doing to ourselves when this disconnect is present. Eating disorders often involve treating ourselves as an object, and attempting to force ourselves to fit into an idealized image of perfection without love and self-care as part of the balance. When someone suffers from an eating disorder, they do not feel enough concern about the damage being done to their body, and are in denial. They are obsessed with food and body image, as if all their value and worth as a person depends on this often unrealistic, idealized image of perfection. In reality, we are not airbrushed before we go out everyday, which are the images in magazines that people sadly compare themselves to.

Many people suffering from eating disorders feel deficient inside, no matter how attractive they are. They never feel good enough, and will do almost anything, including hurting their body to try to fulfill this image of perfection, believing that this is the only way they can feel good about themselves. This is a painful, double bind predicament, and an emotional trap, because from looking through this lens at themselves, the goal of perfection is elusive. People suffering from this are in constant emotional pain, always critically evaluating themselves, and feeling not good enough.

They say to themselves, "I cannot love you, in fact, I will hate you if you don't look like this image I demand of myself." It is crucial to recognize self-hate, and transform it into self-love. While in the throes of an eating disorder, they don't know that through healing, psychotherapy, and support, they can come to peace with themselves. They can learn to take really good care of themselves from the inside out, stop abusing their bodies, and be much more satisfied with life, because they are ultimately healing their relationship with themselves. Feeling worthy, and fulfilling their life goals, in balance, become possible. Eating disorders are very personal and complicated and need to be seen and treated individually, aimed at each person's needs. They are a combination of biochemical, nutritional, emotional, spiritual issue, and neurotransmitter imbalances. I strongly feel that the integrative treatment of eating disorders needs to involve all of these aspects for the healing that is possible. It is learning to nurture your self with love, which is something you can truly have and keep, as you find peace within you with food.

Drug Addiction

When you have a loved one who is suffering from addiction, you and everyone who loves them are suffering too. Every addict has similar underlying issues and causes, however it is necessary to educate yourself about the different signs, symptoms, and side effects that go with each type of addiction. Do you have someone close to you that you are who has never dealt with or recovered from addiction, and you are in a ongoing drama of heartbreak? Many parents and children are in this situation, and everyone's quality of life is compromised.

Addiction is not limited to known substances such as marijuana, cocaine, or ecstasy. According to a CNN report, the new drug, Molly, "is a dangerous combination of unknown chemicals; users have no idea what they are taking or at what dose." Sadly, there have been many deaths due to taking these unknown substances, which come from laboratories in China and are targeted to first time drug users between 12-17 years old.[4] The side effects of Molly can vary. While under the influence of the drug, they may exhibit symptoms of sweating, jaw clenching, violent or bizarre behavior, and psychosis.[5]

Prescription drug addiction is also on the rise and has many complicating factors. Prescription drugs are, on one hand, when used according to directions for a short amount of time can be helpful if necessary. They can also be treacherous because they can be highly addictive, and many people have found themselves addicted to prescription drugs who never thought they would be. Sometimes the trouble could begin in as insidious a way as someone who has been prescribed necessary painkillers for an accident, but then continues to take the medicine long after it is physically necessary. They were vulnerable to this addiction partly due to their physical pain and partly due to their personality. It is crucial for this to be recognized and treated with medical care right away, so they can detox and recover from this prescription use. It is a confusing addiction, because it often starts off with the medicine being prescribed and then ends up with the medicine being used or overused in a harmful way.

Compulsive Gambling and Sex Addictions

Compulsive behaviors like gambling, sex addiction, and internet sex addiction, are, as in all addictions, all greatly problematic. They interfere and wreak destruction in their lives, with heavy negative consequences of

---

[4]Griffin, Drew, et all. "9 Things Everyone Should Know About Molly." CNN. www.cnn.com/2013/11/22/health/9-things-molly-drug. Accessed Nov. 23, 2013. (online)
[5]Ibid

all kinds. These addictions need to be seen and evaluated, as early treatment is essential in order to save someone's life and give them back the chance to have a better quality of life.

Compulsive gamblers cannot stop gambling even at the risk of losing their home, relationship, and job. It is what they think about constantly, even if they know the odds are against them, they impulsively gamble and ignore the consequences. When they are winning or losing, they are caught up in this addiction. There is treatment available, and Gamblers Anonymous has saved many lives from destruction and helped compulsive gamblers gain back their self-respect.

Sex addiction is very similar to a drug addiction, as they are both mechanisms of escape. The addiction stimulates the reward system in the brain, which is what causes the compulsiveness of the behavior. They are pre-occupied by thinking about their next sexual opportunity, and as with all addictions, they are emotionally unavailable to their loved ones, as there is a marked lack of ability to have real intimacy. This addiction causes havoc in one's life and family, and is particularly painful to their significant other. There is much treatment available for sex addiction and internet sex addiction, such as therapy and 12-step meetings, called Sex Addicts Anonymous, which has been powerfully helpful to so many people who are suffering.

*****

Addiction has been referred to as a disease of entitlement, one of self-centeredness, manipulation, and stilted emotional development. Addicts often experience relationship problems, as they are unavailable emotionally, hold toxic secrets, and have low self-esteem. They have an inability to cope with "life on life's terms," as they say in recovery, which means being able to deal constructively with the losses, conflicts, and challenges that life presents.

How many children see their parents act out, over-drink, do drugs, and other inappropriate things? We need to also take an honest and serious look at our own behavior, and the adults that we spend time with, who have influence directly and indirectly over our children. What we teach them by what we demonstrate is powerful. Many children are well aware of their friends' parents drinking, and are often confused by it. All the while that they are trying to develop their own values and boundaries, they are seeing adults who are troubled, and who live in denial of addiction. What effect does that have on them?

Children feel emotionally invisible by the parent who is using. Many parents have missed significant parts of their kids' childhoods by being mood-altered, irritable, high, or blacked out. The child doesn't understand the cause of this, and feels that they did something wrong and that they are not worthy of their parent's attention. The parent who is in the throes of addiction can be unreliable, inconsistent, and children in this situation often don't know who they are coming home to, and if they will be met with love and kindness or screaming and abuse. There are many people who have shared with me that as a child they recall that everyone tensed up and fear flowed through the house when the using parent came home, fearing the unpredictable behavior and moods caused by their addiction.

Conversely, parents who have kids who are using are at first not sure what they are seeing, wondering if it is their teenage moodiness, or if it is more. They wonder if they need to be seriously worried about whether their child is using and hiding it. There are times, when a family is very dysfunctional, in which there are a lack of boundaries and a lack of awareness of the seriousness of what is going on right in front of them; they watch as disastrous consequences begin to arise, such as getting arrested, overdosing, making horribly poor decisions, and getting expelled from school, and aren't able to identify the bigger problem. This, of course, can just as easily happen in a functional family environment. Many times, parents who have created a harmonious, supportive family structure are shocked as well, when their well-adjusted, happy child falls prey to addiction. It can happen in any family. What makes the difference is whether or not the family addresses the issue immediately or is in denial about it. I recall many parents saying that they had their first good night sleep on the first night their kid was sleeping in the rehab facility. After so many months and years of terror about where they were, what they were using, and what kind of trouble they could be in, they knew that for now, their child was safe.

An important aspect of the addiction picture is that the person using does not want to face their own actions as being destructive, and when approached about it, they get very angry and defensive. They often have much shame about it underneath. They may have a tendency for toxic shame. Healthy shame is when the individual faces that they did something wrong, or made a mistake, and then feels the appropriate remorse and sadness. They face the problem, take responsibility for their wrong actions, make amends, and know that they are human. Someone with toxic shame may have made the same mistake, but sees themselves as worthless, and totally invalidates their own being. This shame then causes them to create definitions of alcoholism that disqualifies their own behavior. Such as "I don't drink every day," "I can go a month without drinking," "I go to work everyday and hold down a job," "I'm not passed out on the street," "I can hold a lot of liquor," and "I can even drive because it does not affect me as much as other people." This kind of denial causes deaths everyday. One of the greatest gifts we can give those we love is to have the openness to our own challenges, by facing them, admitting them, and working on ourselves toward being emotionally healthier.

Resistances
People often have many resistances and feel discomfort about

changing their lifestyle to create greater wellness. They often have guilt and anxiety over knowing that they're not eating well and taking good care of themselves, which compounds with the other issues going on in their life, and hook into their habitual negative self-talk.

Do any of these statements sound like you?
"It's too hard."
"There's nothing for me to eat."
"It takes too much time."
"It must be my age. This is what happens when we get older."
"I'll never be successful at (weight loss, eating healthy, healing my issue) so why bother."

When finally coming face to face with the need to change, several defense mechanisms arise as obstacles on their path. These are well-learned behaviors and thinking patterns, stemming from earlier stories about how they deal with the ups and downs of life. To illustrate how these defense mechanisms can affect someone in need of redesigning their eating and wellness plan, I'd like to share with you some examples:

C. came to my office to explore the possibilities available to her to improve her wellness. She was experiencing aches and pains which were in the process of being diagnosed by her Primary Care physician as osteoarthritis. She had more fatigue and felt less vital than she remembered from her earlier years. She is only in her 40s, but believes that the symptoms she has are based on her age. Sadly, this is a belief system that many people have. Our minds make up a reason why we are experiencing symptoms, even though they are really a reflection of our nutritional imbalances, which can create an inflammatory process in our bodies. I have learned that when inflammation starts, it goes everywhere. Inflammation is part of the basis of all degenerative conditions and it's especially important to focus on its reduction. The opposite of that is true also: when inflammation declines, it improves everywhere in the body, as well.

C. was also experiencing sleep issues in which she was waking up often throughout the night and feeling tired in the morning. She had a very high-stress job, and was not managing stress physiologically or emotionally well. It was getting to her and she was in tears. This is where nutrition and psychology intersect. Even though she wanted to improve her health badly, at the beginning of our work together, she was not connected to how to make the real changes needed. She related to me a recent struggle in which she was thinking that she really wanted to be healthier, but she was rushing around and she "didn't think, and I grabbed something that wasn't really good for me. And then I felt really bad and frustrated afterwards."

This is self-destructive and does not honor her deeper longing and wishes for creating greater health. One powerful realization we can come to is that we have the strength to defy what is negative and enhance what is positive and life affirming for us. This is truly the beginning of empowerment. Change is not solely a rational process. It is also an emotional and attitudinal shift that often needs support for the underlying emotions that get in the way. C. had a history of doing the same things over and over again, which did not create the outcome she had been looking for. She had always wanted to have a smaller waist and a flat stomach, and she was often very uncomfortable buying clothes, as she greatly focused on the excess weight around her mid-section. She continually attempted to lose this weight by going on very restrictive diets that made her feel very deprived and miserable. Invariably, she would begin to see some results, but could not sustain the rigidity and deprivation of the eating plans, and she would fall off the diet. This resulted in frustration and hopelessness at her seeming inability to lose weight and to be at peace with her body.

These emotions would then led her to go through periods of paying very little care and attention to what she ate, and gain the weight back, a process which would be counterproductive to her longing for success. Her negative self-talk and criticism sabotaged her original intentions and she unconsciously punished herself by acting out in a careless way towards herself, and it hurt her self-esteem even further.

Every action we take is based on a decision, and the more conscious we become of our inner self-talk and the directives we give ourselves, the more we can influence our behavior.

Another aspect of C.'s predicament was her lack of motivation and procrastination when it came to going to the gym that she had spent a great deal of money on. She had reasoned that not only would it be great for her to start exercising regularly, but that if she were paying so much money, she would feel compelled to go. However, her overriding defense mechanisms kicked in and she continually found reasons not to go. Whether she was too tired, didn't have enough time, didn't feel well, or didn't have any clean workout clothes available, she started finding that the times she went to the gym grew fewer and fewer. This also caused her much distress, because she not only felt like a failure for not working out, but she was wasting tremendous amounts of money. Up until this time, C. had no idea that such a concept as self-care even existed.

"Self-care is the one need that no one can afford to ignore."
—Deepak Chopra

Socially, C. is often around people who are not eating well. When they see that she is beginning a new way of relating to food, they question her new choices instead of supporting her. They feel threatened by her desire to be healthier and her new eating choices.

C. is now in the process of mending unhealed hurts deep in her core self, gaining a healthier self-respect, and restoring her dignity, as she learns to incorporate true lasting self-care, which is love in action.

While many people can relate to C.'s story, there are other dangers of not paying attention to nutritional and psychological wellness.

Years ago, another client, R., was referred to my office for depression and anxiety issues. She had great difficulty in romantic relationships and always seemed to pick dysfunctional, self-centered men who had a lack of empathy and real concern for her. As much as they felt entitled, she felt unentitled. She was drawn to men who were looking for someone who was compliant, forgiving, and patient to an extreme. Her harmful co-dependency was a perfect fit for damaging, critical men. She was overly attuned to the care of others and especially the man in her life, and she would excuse and rationalize to herself their mean and insensitive behavior. She suffered from low self-esteem, lack of healthy boundaries, and poor self-care, both emotionally and nutritionally. R. had many inner gifts and great potential that were clearly evident to me, but not to her.

One of the reasons R. suffered so much was due to the learned defense mechanisms, brought on by childhood wounds that led to her co-dependency, in which she would over-give to others while sacrificing herself and her own needs on a very deep level. Defense mechanisms function to self-protect ourselves from pain, however they can also cause much damage by preventing us from facing the truth of what's really going on and the sanctions necessary to truly address conflicts. These mechanisms are often a way to excuse or neutralize what is happening so we really don't have to deal with it, change it, or actualize it.

One of the most common defense mechanisms is rationalism, in which we create an explanation in our minds of why something unacceptable is really OK with us. It continually excuses the behavior of either ourselves or another person, and prevents us from embracing our true feelings, our pain, and how deeply offended we might be. It's a way of disconnecting and being out of touch with our true self.

Rationalizations appear in our inner dialogue where we will often have a debate with ourselves about how we will deal with a conflicting or upsetting situation, such as being lied to, betrayed, hurt, insulted, and disrespected. In R.'s case, when the men in her life would not keep their word to her, break promises, not show up on time, flirt with other women in front of her, lie about where they were on a certain night, use drugs, or see an old girlfriend, they would lie to her and she would come up with a logical reason why they would be late, or seemed suspicious. The people who do the lying in the first place, rationalize to themselves that they are doing so in order to protect their partner from hurt. But in the case of R., and many others like her, hurt is inevitable. In reality, this is a selfish, cowardly act of trying to control the outcome after the initial decision to act out in a harmful way. By lying about it, they take the right of R. and others to have their own feelings, experiences, and conclusions based on the truth of what they need to do for themselves. By then rationalizing the bad behavior of another, the co-dependent person themselves goes into denial in order to keep the relationship going, often blaming themselves for the issues in the relationship.

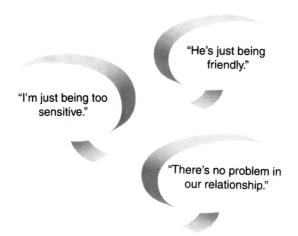

"He's just being friendly."

"I'm just being too sensitive."

"There's no problem in our relationship."

Denial, another defense mechanism, arises when one has the sense that something doesn't feel right, but they don't trust themselves, and they tell their self that they are just making a big deal out of nothing.

Denial occurs when a person **doubts** their own reality and then **denies** their own reality. It is a conscious or unconscious refusal to acknowledge an unacceptable and/or uncomfortable truth or emotion, or to admit it to our self. Denial literally influences us in a way that we cannot see what we are doing to our health, our mind, and our body. The unconscious doesn't know the word "not." Our head spins, doubting ourselves and doubting what we just saw. Denial is coming to the conclusion that what we saw or experienced didn't really happen, even though there is proof that something did happen. The clues are there but we deny that they have any meaning.

R. was in denial about her partner's deceit and destructive behavior, which led to emotional pain, which then led to her pattern of overeating when in distress. She would also be highly self-critical and doubt her own decisions. She had stopped paying attention to what she was eating, which resulted in nutrient depletion, depression, and further anxiety, because her body could not make the healthy chemicals we need for mental and physical stability. She also began smoking again after years of having stopped. R. began messing up at work, as she was preoccupied and in a constant state of high stress, and her work quality started to decline. This led to further consequences, as she was put on warning about her work quality diminishing. She felt shame about this and isolated herself at a time when she most needed real support and love around her. She kept returning to the dysfunctional man in her life, hoping to get the emotional support she needed, but he was unable to provide. No matter how hard she tried to explain what her needs were and why she was so hurt at times, she was never able to get through to him and be understood. R. had created an impossible no-win situation in which she continued to blame herself. She would interpret his rejection of her as her own fault and a sign of her innate unworthiness of love.

The origins of the feeling of being unworthy of love, which had created the codependency, stemmed directly from a repressed or suppressed pain from a childhood situation; one in which she viewed herself as to blame for the difficulties of her parents and unworthy of their love and support. The definition of repression is a shutting down of a past memory that is very painful in order to prevent anxiety and deep emotion pain. By repressing old painful memories, our unconscious mind is attempting to protect us from the memories we are afraid of knowing or remembering. However, these memories often get triggered by present day events, which create new traumas to deal with. The conscious version of this mechanism is called suppression. The painful memories and experiences are "stuffed" inside consciously in order to protect oneself from the pain.

I realized very quickly, when working with R., that she was repressing the memories of how as a child she would need to neutralize her father's critical, cold communication with her, and his lack of empathy. She then had to rationalize his lack of warmth and emotional unavailability by reasoning that he was so smart, and worked so hard, that she was asking too much from him and was too needy. She then began to perceive herself as too needy, and she repressed her anger and her disappointment of her father. It was much more acceptable for her to unconsciously blame herself than to see or feel how unloved she felt by her father. That identification created her lifelong pattern of seeking out emotionally unavailable partners who would reinforce that view of herself. She would stay with these men, because she would feel lost when she was not in a relationship, and out of her inability to trust her own assessment of the situation and make empowered decisions based on it. She also would avoid any conflicts that could lead to separation, because of her fear of being abandoned by men, as her father had emotionally abandoned her.

If you can relate to R.'s situation, please know that you can heal co-dependent behavior, through therapy and specialized programs. Begin by making a commitment to learning how to like and love yourself by standing up for yourself and what feels right and true for you. Compassion and empathy for your journey leads to greater emotional wellness, and can bring more confidence and self-respect along with it.

Another client, S., came to my office as a last hope before considering gastric bypass surgery for weight loss. She had struggled all her life with a weight problem and was suffering acutely. She was a compulsive and emotional eater, and she had not learned to cope with painful feelings, and so used food as her numbing drug. She had been suffering from metabolic syndrome, nutritional imbalances, cravings, and underlying depression and anxiety. S. came from a very dysfunctional family, where there was poor communication and she felt very emotionally isolated and never had her young psychological needs met. She created a pseudo-solution for her loneliness and emptiness by turning to food for comfort and solace. This really turned into a full-blown compulsive eating addiction. The more weight she had gained, the sadder and more hopeless she became.

S. also had a deep feeling of being trapped in her body and had fleeting images of what her body would be like if she was her ideal weight; this dissonance caused much emotional pain, as she did not feel able to put a plan into action and live it in the reality of her everyday life. That's why she wanted to have gastric bypass surgery. She didn't believe her mind, body, or spirit could make this change after years of deep frustration and pain.

This also manifested in her feeling isolated as an adult and choosing to eat only when she was alone. She had so much shame about her eating and weight that she did not want to be around other people in social situations, and she believed she needed to hide her addictive and secret eating from the world. She longed deep down for friendships and a love relationship, but she didn't believe they would be possible for her. Projection, as a defense mechanism, is when a person subconsciously denies her or her own negative attributes by assigning them instead to the outside world. She projected her own internal feelings of rejection onto the men that she did meet and was interested in. She assumed that they couldn't find her attractive because she didn't find herself attractive.

S. had been on many diets that were short-lived, rigid, and depriving. She felt that since she kept failing at losing weight, she believed that it wasn't possible for her. S. was projecting her inability to lose weight and be at peace and alignment with her body now and in the future.

She then committed herself to deep consistent psychotherapy, addressing the underlying issues that had never really been dealt with before in the way they needed to be. Just because something happened long ago, doesn't mean it is resolved, or that it doesn't deserve psychological attention at present. This is another way that many people short-circuit their growth. For example, they may say to themselves, "It happened so long ago, I should have gotten over it already," or a loved one saying, "It's in the past, get over it, move forward." Many times we cannot move forward from a significant hurt from our past, unless it gets the healing attention and care it deserves. Then the gaping wound becomes incorporated into the life experience of the person, and becomes a more healed scar. S. also attended Overeaters Anonymous meetings in conjunction with therapy, that provided much support, empathy, and connection which she deeply needed.

Another patient, B., was referred to my office from his gastroenterologist due to severe constipation. He was in his mid-40s and had been suffering for about six years. He always felt bloated and had inflammation in his joints. He was rarely able to eliminate, often less than once a month and only with stimulant laxatives. He was deeply sad, stressed, and depressed. He had low energy, fatigue, and poor quality sleep. He was missing out on many activities he wished he could participate in. This problem was affecting every area of his life, and was constantly on his mind. B. was involved with a career involving much travel, which he had to suspend. He had lost interest in the activities he had, and did not pursue any new ones, as he had lost faith in his body being able to work properly. He had been given strong pharmaceuticals, which had many side effects and had made him feel sick. He was truly traumatized by his problem. When we began our journey, he was very eager and motivated to get better, although very skeptical that this could really work, because he had tried so many things.

B. had a lot of fear and anxiety about his future, and doubted that he would ever be well. In addition, he had Obsessive Compulsive Disorder (OCD), which caused greater anxiety because people with OCD struggle to control their world by thoughts or behaviors that aim to make their world safe. The interesting connection between B.'s constipation problems and his OCD, is that both represent a "stuckness" of the mind and body. Unconsciously, B. had been eating things that contributed to his constipation and had had a very rigid relationship with food. He had a very limited range of foods he would eat, and that went with his self-imposed restrictions in the rest of his life. The consequent reaction of his body with constipation created a further fear of eating anything new.

He didn't know how to properly nourish himself, both emotionally and physically, and always chose foods that were nutrient-deficient and highly processed. He believed that something was terribly wrong with him.

The defense mechanism of isolation, is used when a person feels unable to fully participate in the world, and so feels safer when they are alone. B. was isolated from being able to work and didn't feel as if he could go out and have a social life, as he was constantly worrying about not being able to go to the bathroom and whether his body would function properly.

B. began to work on himself, making dietary changes, taking special nutrients, and focusing on his emotional healing. His body began responding positively almost immediately, giving him hope and confidence that this was working. He is a different man today, with much more health, freedom, and confidence to live his life more fully, and is back to the traveling that he loves.

Ironically, people can't seem to get rid of what they don't want, like weight or a health condition, but they often lose what they do want to hold on to, like money, their job, or their relationship, resulting in feelings of sadness and frustration.

Normalizing Symptoms

> "A long habit of not thinking a thing wrong, gives it
> a superficial appearance of being right."
> —Thomas Paine, *Common Sense*

One psychological phenomenon that I have universally observed, is how many people normalize their symptoms by giving them a seemingly rational, "out of their control" reason. We see many people suffering from conditions, and we often think, "Well, that is what happens when you age," even if they are thirty-five years old. They think, "I must have this because of my age, or it's my genetics, or this is what happens after menopause."

These things are often not true, and real changes in nutrition, lifestyle, psychology, and empowerment can make all the difference in our improvement of life. Our thinking guides us and our lifestyle follows, which totally affects the quality of our life and health. Most conditions today that people suffer from are lifestyle-related, and can be greatly improved by making empowered choices for health. I have seen many people say that their health and weight are better in their 60s and 70s than they were in their 30s and 40s.

Children's Psychological Health

Parenting is such an amazing life challenge, as not only are we trying to be as healthy as possible for ourselves, accepting our own difficulties and imperfections, it is crucial for us to be emotionally healthy while we have the sacred duty of bringing up our children. We want them to be able to figure out who they are as individuals, and see their own value as a human being. Children have very powerful feelings about their parents being authentic with them, and will see through where we are not being honest.

Children are also powerful teachers for us, who throw us curves, push our deepest buttons, and at times, challenge us all the way.

Self-Esteem/Self-Respect

Our emotional health and wellness totally impacts how our kids feel about themselves. One of the most pertinent factors of why effective and constructive parenting is so crucial, is because kids internalize deep messages from us, which then form their identity, and their developing self-concept about themselves. This begins pre-verbally, and becomes part of their psyche for the rest of their lives.

As developing beings, children need to see in their parents a mirror of their inherent goodness, lovability, their potential, and the freedom to develop into, and be respected for, who they truly are. At the same time, children need healthy boundaries to keep them safe and to learn how to construct their own boundaries for their own lives and ongoing development. Healthy boundaries prevent suffering. They teach us right from wrong behaviors, how to treat ourselves, and others, and how we allow others to treat us. Having healthy boundaries empowers us to say no or yes with wisdom, confidence, and self-respect. This is the lens that they will look through and that will affect every decision that they make, and it becomes the foundation of our feelings of self-worth and self-esteem.

This is the beginning of learning self-care and self-responsibility. This is also the core of seeing ourselves in a balanced way, knowing our gifts, our difficulties, and our vulnerabilities, able to see that we are worthwhile beings who can continue to grow and learn.

Technology Challenges and Guidelines

We, as parents, are in a new world of technology. Parents are stressed and unsure how to deal with how to regulate their kids' use of screens, and finding balance in their lives. It's not easy for parents, because technology is so incredibly attractive to kids, that they often avoid other activities that are so important for their development. Kids often know so much more than we do in the area of technology, and they pick it up more quickly than we do, which presents so many obstacles for parents and kids to have to work out.

For example, during a family discussion or argument, you find out that one of your kids is on FaceTime with their friends, and so broadcasting your argument or family business to others. A recording of you yelling at your child in a moment of frustration could be simultaneously sent out to your kid's friends and/or to social media. Kids have not yet developed good judgment or healthy boundaries in what is appropriate to send out to the world, and some of what they do exchange could be very upsetting to parents. They need our supervision and our guidance. There are many more stories and examples of this dilemma.

Some questions and thoughts to ponder:

1. Are your kids looking at while you are speaking to them? You could be at the dinner table, or sitting with them on the couch and their eyes are glued to their electronic devices.

2. Does this happen while you are driving them somewhere and trying to have a conversation with them? They are often in the back seat looking at their devices and not even listening to you. The parent is telling their child something important, or simply asking how their day was. The parent may see this as an opportunity for a meaningful exchange, but the problem with this is that your kids are, at best, only half listening to you. At some point, you realize that they are not really listening to you at all. One way that many parents come to realize that their kids weren't really listening is when they seem to have no recollection of something the parent had told them. Our brains weren't made to multi-task and it can take a big toll on us. Unless you and your kids have a prearranged agreement that while you are having a conversation, their screens are off, you risk their inattentiveness.

3. Do you know how many hours a day your kids are online? You might be surprised. By first realizing exactly how much time your child is online, or on a device, you can help to regulate their use of technology.

4. Do they rush through dinner or homework to get back to their devices? Again, by regulating the hours that they can use their devices, you can ensure a more relaxed dinner, with hopefully conversation and eye contact.

5. Do you know what content they are looking at, either sent from someone else or while playing in a game? Parents need to be more

aware of the things their child is looking at on their devices. Some of the material could be violent or otherwise inappropriate.

6. What ages do we allow kids to play very violent video games that are marked for 17 and over? Many younger kids are now playing these violent and suggestive games. What effect are these games having on our kids? There are great concerns about violent games lessening their empathy and compassion, and desensitizing their reaction to violence. This can also lead to a lack of overall relatedness to others, less ability to communicate and express oneself directly, and a difficulty with being in tune with one's own emotions.

7. How many hours are your kids sleeping? This is a huge issue. Many kids are over-stimulated by their use of online activities, such as YouTube, video games, instant messaging with friends, Instagram, etc., late into the night, unless monitored. Even if their bodies are truly tired, they don't experience their need for sleep; however, over time, they suffer from many of the symptoms of lack of sleep, such as not being able to get up in the morning, feeling in a fog for the first few periods of the school day, having less concentration and focus, and increased irritability and mood disorders, to name a few. The combination of sleep deprivation, depression, poor nutrition, and a lack of physical exercise take a tremendous toll on our kids and can interfere with their optimal development.

Here are some helpful solutions:
1. Plug your child's electronic devices into a room other than their bedroom. You will be protecting them from both electromagnetic fields and from the temptation of looking at screens under the covers, long after parents are asleep.
2. Have an agreement with your kids about the time that screens are put away for the night, and plugged in. Teach them good sleep

hygiene, in which there is a pre-sleep period where they can read a book in bed, or listen to soft music, or just relax, which gives our mind and body the message to slow down and become sleepy.

3. Help your kids to have a balance in their daily activities, with technology having a place within it, but not a totally dominating force. This will help to guard against technology addictions.

Accountability

It is important to create accountability in our children. One example is to give them the "driving rap" as early as possible, by informing your children at younger ages that simply turning the age of 18 (or 16, depending on the location), is only one necessary factor in their being allowed to drive. We need to impart the concept that driving is not their birthright, it is a privilege that they can earn though their responsible actions, their demonstrations of impulse control, and by making constructive decisions.

The last thing we want to do to our children is to spoil them to the point that they feel entitled, have no self-discipline, no respect, and are totally self-centered and self-indulgent. If this sounds familiar, you are not alone, and it is important for parents to know that there is much you can do about it. Children need to learn and to develop the capacity to become responsible in every area of their life. Limiting and regulating screen time is often necessary, and in the long run, can be greatly helpful in your children' development. They do not have the inner discipline or inner structure to regulate this for themselves. They need us, their parents, to set the healthy boundaries, so they can eventually internalize the empowering ability to set those boundaries for themselves as they mature. This can help to protect them from the lure of addictive behaviors.

Our perceptions of life are formed by our conscious and unconscious emotional and physical experiences. From intrauterine to conscious speaking in sentences, we have a feeling about our lives and ourselves.

This is a perceptual lens we see through that colors our vision and what we believe. What is amazing is that we often do not realize we are looking through a colored lens, but think that it is reality we are seeing. This is a powerful crossroads in our human journey. What we perceive about our self, and our view of our past and our future, lies in a place of deep feeling that swirls inside us and seeps up at inopportune moments. We might have a swell of feelings like a tsunami in reaction mode, as we make assumptions about what is going on in ourselves and others, only to find out that we misunderstood or misperceived a situation and reacted strongly based on those conclusions, often made in just a split second. Therapy is learning to see what we do not see about ourselves. This enables us to have a more balanced perception, so that we can identify our own feelings and reactions with empowered awareness of what's really happening. Part of this is being able to see the other person's perception, as well, so that we can embrace both with compassion and openness, and come to a balanced and clear understanding of the situation, which then allows us to feel connected to our truth. This process creates relatedness, an integral part of love. Understanding and integrating another's point of view and reality can add to our own insight of the situation and ourselves. It's giving breath to another point of view and another possibility.

The Biology of Wellness: Taking it to a Deeper Level

Chapter Four

"The food you eat can either be the safest and most powerful
form of medicine, or the slowest form of poison."
—Ann Wigmore, *The Hippocrates Diet and Health Program*

There is an inner battle playing out within us, between our biochemistry, our mind, and our body; a conflict over the paradoxical chasm between the mental urges of physical and emotional cravings, and our bodies' true physiological and nutritional needs. The mental urges and the real needs argue like a debate team, each trying to reason and win their point. We develop patterns of thinking and further develop habitual thoughts, and then repeat them over and over again. Without realizing it, we are conning ourselves. Meanwhile, our inner self has its own goals, dreams, and desires for greater health and wellness that often get ignored, as our ingrained patterns shout over that inner voice of truth.

It's like an adolescent having a "but I want to" moment, to which a parent then responds to with a determined, "NO." The inner adolescent then tries to change their parent's decision from a "no" to a "yes." This pubescent part of our mind jumps into action, as if it had just taken a high level course in powerful, mind-altering, subliminal techniques, while achieving an emotional black belt in aikido! This skilled manipulation technique then executes a series of inner debates, each one hooking on to the next level, attempting to move the parent along the continuum from something that the parent was originally completely against, to finding themselves agreeing with the teenager's wants, thus allowing the adolescent's perfectly executed plan to convince their parents and to be successful in getting what they want. This is what we do to ourselves internally. It sets up a fertile ground in our minds to repeat this repetitive pattern again and again, strengthening its power over us. There is an undercurrent of awareness of this very specific series of thoughts that culminates in "I went off track and I don't know why;" almost as if we don't realize how many thoughts went into this complex process of fighting with and fooling ourselves. No wonder we get exhausted just from the mental gymnastics of this dynamic. We apply similar techniques to ourselves if we are responding destructively to our own cravings, even if we know what we are considering will create negative consequences. How we fool ourselves cannot be too direct, however, or conning ourselves will not work as well. This destructive inner sabotage can go on repeatedly, and the suffering it results in will take precious time to recover from. How we take care of ourselves psychologically, our thoughts and our beliefs, applied to our nutritional life style, affects every other process in our bodies and in our lives.

What does our hidden destructive psychology impacting our biochemistry look like in action? It can look like this: You have been making lifestyle changes and notice that when you do, you are feeling better and having more energy. Then, one day, you are feeling tired and stressed from many different directions that have been building up inside you and need your attention. You then find yourself thinking, "I want something to eat. What should I have that's healthy? I know! I'll have an apple!" You go and look at the apples in your fridge, successfully getting yourself to be standing in front of the fridge with the door open, staring at what's in there. The next thought becomes, "I had apples and other fruits already today, what else can I have that's like an apple?" You see apple butter, perhaps, or you see dried apples, and you tell yourself that they're too sweet. Then your mind swings around to what it was secretly originally aiming for - the apple pie that someone brought that you did not want in your house, but has been, nevertheless, lingering in your refrigerator like a lingering thought in your mind. You have had a stressful day, and you know you feel so much better without sugar, wheat, and all the stuff that is in this apple pie. It would be wise to say no, since deep down you know you are not going to be okay with this rash decision, physically or emotionally. You have begun to be seduced by this tricky inner pull, and the longer you stare at the pie, the inner debate chaos goes on within. To make matters more complicated, physiological changes are now taking place. How stressful!

So here's what happens next…first, the inner remorse sets in, then the fatigue sets in from the physical effects of the wheat, sugar, and unhealthy oils in this pie that the new you didn't really want to eat. Why do we keep doing this to ourselves?

One component of this issue is the myriad of psychological factors discussed in the previous chapter. But there are physiological issues at play as well. I believe in getting rid of cravings biochemically, instead of fighting them. I know this is possible from helping many people do this and it is a hidden key in finding peace and freedom within. Since I do not believe in deprivation, one positive alternative is to make something from scratch with apples, cinnamon, and other healthy ingredients. This can be delicious and satisfying, without the ingredients that you know your body feels so much better without. A very important self-communication with our mind and body is registering your body's response to what agrees with you and what doesn't. Most people know what foods make them feel bad. The question really is, are you going to become sensitive to what your body is really showing you? Connecting to this will help you grow in the wisdom of caring for your body. Planning and preparing food that you enjoy and is healthy for you, creates a harmonious feeling within. The solution lies in a paradigm shift, of being loving to yourself, and creative, rather than feeling deprived and rigid, which only works against you. What we become aware of today, and we can begin to envision in our mind, body, and cellular knowledge, can be the beginning of significant change in our lives. This process can become a catalyst to bring us toward greater wellness.

The following conditions mentioned are intended to illustrate the effect of our nutrition on our wellness.

ADD/ADHD

Many kids these days are having symptoms such as impulsivity, inattention, difficulty focusing, and hyper-activity. They are often easily distracted, miss important details, and have difficulty organizing themselves.

The missing element in a more complete treatment for ADD or ADHD, is looking at the child's diet. From my experience, a huge contributing factor to this condition is the consumption of processed food, fast food, deep-fried food, sodas, high sugar, artificially-colored sports drinks, high-fructose corn syrup, hydrogenated fats, partially hydrogenated fats, and unhealthy oils. Poor nutrition and highly processed foods have a negative impact on brain chemistry and can worsen symptoms a child is experiencing.

Adrenal Health

If your adrenal glands could talk to you, what would they be saying? Our adrenals are there to help provide us with the strength and ability to deal with stressful situations. When under acute stress, our bodies produce adrenaline and cortisol, hormones that are part of our sympathetic nervous system, which help us have the strength to get out of danger and handle extreme stress.

We also need our parasympathetic nervous system to function well, because this creates soothing, relaxing calm to our system. Our nervous system creates our own bio-chemicals like GABA and serotonin to create a balance with our sympathetic nervous system, which ramps us up. The systems of our bodies all need balance so that they can work in a beautiful synergy to keep us resilient and well. It is crucial, therefore, to work on our nutritional lifestyle to help repair and prevent adrenal burnout and fatigue. More on these hormones in the next section on brain health.

It is a combination of our nutrition, psychology, and spirituality that keep our adrenals healthy. If the right questions aren't being asked, many people who are hurting will fall through the cracks in their doctors' offices. What is really going on in your life? What is worrying you the most? What do you fear? Are you in a toxic relationship? What is hurting deep inside? What do you most need? The true needs of a person can be met by looking at the whole being. This person might need a referral to an excellent therapist, nutritionist, massage therapist (being touched with loving care is something that many people are starving for), or other therapies that are appropriate, but it is crucial to work on our lifestyle nutritionally in order to help repair and prevent adrenal burnout and fatigue. To be able to produce hormones in all of our body's systems we need to be well nourished.

Presenting recently at a women's conference, many women admitted to me that their "nutrition is terrible." This greatly concerns me. There are so many people walking around like this, not connecting the dots to the far-reaching effects and dire consequences of poor nutrition. Those people need to be reached. The people who are not getting the help they need; those who are suffering, often in hidden ways. They need to be empowered so they can find real-life solutions to their challenges.

To keep our nervous system working properly, we need to be well nourished with all the raw materials that healthy eating provides. Our bodies need to be able to help us adapt with resilience to stressors. We need nutrients that support adrenal health, like B-vitamins, magnesium, whole food antioxidants, and essential minerals. If our adrenals, which are the emergency broadcasting system of our body, are exhausted and on overload this is a symptom that we need support and healing. Self-care is crucial to how we adapt to the stress in our lives. We need to keep nursing and protecting our adrenals from all stressors of body, mind, and spirit. We need to connect to our deeper wisdom and intuition, which leads to loving self-care through our nutrition. We need to have deep and excellent sleep, and if we are not sleeping well, we need to address that.

Our emotional health has a profound effect on our adrenal health. Our adrenals are sitting there on our kidneys ready to help us, and they need our loving attention. Chronic emotional stress can affect us, and put us at a higher risk for illness.

Adrenal fatigue can be a wake up call, a signal that we need to connect to ourselves on a deeper level, and figure out how to bring healing into our lives. When under stress, our adrenals react, and we are actually produce increased stress hormones like cortisol, adrenaline, and norepinephrine. When we go into high stress mode, or "fight or flight," our adrenals attempt to help us adapt to the stressful situation we are facing. If it is temporary stress going on and can be easily resolved, our flight or flight response helps us and isn't harmful. But if the stress turns into high chronic stress, the extended period of elevated stress hormones can do serious damage to our brain and body. This can turn into adrenal fatigue and burnout. It is crucial to look at how our psychology impacts our adrenal health, and how it impacts our biology as a whole.

Brain Health and Neurotransmitters

Brain health is so essential that, in theory, we should be doing anything we can to keep our brain healthy. But do we, in actuality? Brain health involves the cognitive side, involving memory, clarity, and problem solving, and the emotional side, of emotions and feelings. When it comes to anti-aging, illness prevention, and the desire to have a long vital life, we need our brain to be well nourished.

Our brains are the control centers of our body, and need our loving care and attention! Do you ever think about your neurotransmitters? It might sound strange, but if you ever wonder about why you are feeling cranky, irritable, craving sweets, unable to sleep, or depressed you are questioning your neurotransmitters. There are four main neurotransmitters that affect our mood: serotonin, dopamine, GABA, and norepinephrine. As all of the systems of our bodies need balance, this is especially true of our inhibitory and excitatory neurotransmitters. They are like the gas pedal and the brake of the brain. We would be in big trouble if we were driving a car without the gas pedal and the brake working in synergy with each other. It is the same with our brain and nervous system.

Our inhibitory neurotransmitters, serotonin, GABA, and dopamine, are calming and quiet things down in us. GABA is a major inhibitory neurotransmitter, and is a soothing agent of our brain. GABA helps us to reduce anxiety and make us more resilient to stress, and also helps regulate our mood. Serotonin is an inhibitory neurotransmitter connected to feeling happiness, and it helps us to be less vulnerable to depression, sadness, and anxiety. In this day and age, when depression and anxiety seem to be rampant, it helps us to keep a calm mood and stable brain. Some symptoms of serotonin depletion are poor sleep, sugar and carbohydrate cravings, low mood, a poor immune system, low energy, an irritable attitude, and digestive problems. Dopamine is a neurotransmitter that is connected to the reward center of our brain. It provides a sense of pleasure and satisfaction.

The excitatory neurotransmitters are adrenaline, epinephrine, and norepinephrine. Excitatory neurotransmitters are like putting our foot on the gas pedal. They ramp us up, and get us focused and ready to take on the challenges before us. They keep us fired up to do the task at hand, but they only work well if our inhibitory neurotransmitters are also available to keep the balance, so that we don't get too hyper, stressed, or anxious. It's like working hard all day with focus and drive and being productive, and then in the evening we give ourselves the message that it is time to unwind and relax. Then it's the time for soothing and calming neurotransmitters to flow, slowing down the excitatory signals, and allowing for relaxation, moving us toward a wonderful night's sleep. This ideal picture is when excitatory and inhibitory are working well together. However, if this is not the case for you, it is important to recognize and learn what you can do to improve your important brain balance.

My experience has been, when seeing people who are feeling irritable, have cravings for addictive substances, an increase in anger and aggression, and/or cravings for cigarettes, that they most likely have a neurotransmitter imbalance. Neurotransmitters are meant to work in symphony with each other, in order to create balanced brain chemistry, which, in turn, provides a greater sense of wellbeing.

The good news is that our brains can improve their functioning and heal in many ways. Improving our brain chemistry involves making a commitment to improving our nutrition and crucial lifestyle elements such as: sleep, hydration, exercise, nutrients, and therapy. One suggestion for better brain health would be to lessen the use of caffeine in our diets. Excess caffeine can give us jitters, make us nervous, contribute to insomnia, and deplete our serotonin. Another suggestion would be to lessen our use of alcohol, if we are drinking in excess. Even one four-ounce glass negatively impacts our brain, contributing to neurotransmitter imbalance, insomnia, and depression. What do you think your body is trying to tell you when you are hung over? People have told me for many years how lousy they feel the next few days after over-drinking. An important fact to know is that within thirty seconds of ingesting alcohol, it is already affecting our brain and our liver.

Another crucial aspect of brain health depletion is a poor diet, due to a lack of nutrients, vitamins, minerals, and essential fatty acids. The first step in improving our brain health is to improve our nutrition, even if a doctor has never asked you what you eat in a detailed way. *I am asking you....* If you want to have a healthier brain, it's best to stay away from toxic substances, such as heavy metals, pesticides, drugs, alcohol (as mentioned earlier), MSG (monosodium glutamate) in all its forms, bad oils, excititoxins like artificial sweeteners, processed foods, and deep fried foods.

Create a healthy life program for yourself, for which I have provided some guidelines in Chapter Eight. Include more whole foods in your diet. Fruits and vegetables are filled with antioxidants and they help protect our brains from excess oxidative stress and free radical attack, which can damage our neurons. Make sure you eat plenty of fresh plant-based food, as much as you can. There are so many beautiful foods from nature, like mixed greens, avocados, nuts and seeds, legumes, fresh herbs and spices, sprouts, micro greens, lemons, garlic, onions, broccoli, and other fruits and vegetables that are delicious, protective, and visually beautiful.

Addiction

When we use destructive substances or participate in unhealthy behaviors it is because we do not want to feel our feelings. We hope to avoid emotional pain, emptiness, and uncomfortable emotions, and have a desire to feel better, as we discussed in the last chapter on psychology. But there is a biological component to addiction.

Having depleted or imbalanced brain chemicals can leave us vulnerable to cravings of all sorts. Addiction is an emotional, biological, and spiritual condition that needs attention on all of these levels to fully approach recovery. Some factors that can impact one's vulnerability to addiction are genetic pre-disposition and the chemical reactions created by introductory drug use. At some point, the neurotransmitter reaction to the substance takes over and wants more, sometimes devoid of a psychological need for more of the substance. It is certainly a complex issue. Recovery is a depth-full process; it is not simply about stopping the use of unhealthy substances, even if that were possible. When our brains are depleted, we become irritable and crave soothing. If we do not recognize the need to nourish our brains, we can go in very destructive directions. Facing addiction takes courage, and can ultimately save your life.

It is also greatly helpful to become sober with food. Long ago, in Overeaters Anonymous, someone figured out that being sober with food meant eliminating sugar, white flour, and processed food, similar to an alcoholic being sober from alcohol. It is true that sugar can cause everything in your stomach to ferment, creating a kind of alcohol effect, which is why many people doze off, feeling sleepy, or become very hyper after ingesting sugar. I know there was real wisdom in this at OA, because these substances are not only highly addictive, but they create increased cravings and imbalance our neurotransmitters. They then get totally tangled up with our emotional confusion with food and overeating and off we go on a wild rollercoaster ride. But, there is a way out. Real lasting healing is possible if you are willing to do the work. Transforming your nutrition will pay off for the rest of your life, and set you free from the substances that have been plaguing you.

Gluten Sensitivity

Many people are suffering from the effects of gluten, in numerous aspects of their health. Since they have not been diagnosed with celiac, they may not realize that they are being affected. Symptoms of gluten sensitivity include: gut problems, thyroid issues, depression, inflammation, brain fog, and brain disruption, to name a few. There has been much information and research recently on problems with gluten.

Constipation and Gut Health

I was talking with a gastroenterologist who regularly refers patients to me with complex problems; they are often severely constipated and in need of nutritional intervention and psychotherapy. I told him that I love helping constipated people! They were suffering, and I love helping people to see their body begin working in a way that they had stopped believing was possible.

Constipation is often caused by lifestyle-related difficulties, like eating highly processed, de-natured food without naturally occurring whole food fiber, and foods that lack essential macro- and micronutrients. A whole foods diet with fresh foods is needed for vitality, rather than processed foods, which lead to toxicity in the form of chronic constipation, sluggishness, bloating, and fatigue. There is also a significant connection to the toxicity that occurs when people do not eliminate properly, and lose touch with this part of themselves that is crucial for detoxification. They also begin to lose faith in their own body ever being capable of working properly again, which is part of the ongoing trauma of having chronic constipation. Constipation affects one's mood negatively, contributing to depression and irritability. Constipation can also contribute to many other bowel disorders, and an increased risk of different types of cancers. So the more processed, lifeless, low-fiber food, lack of fruits and vegetables and healthy life-giving foods, the higher our risk is for inadequate elimination, slower motility, weaker peristalsis, and a build up of toxins that affect our total health picture. People who are chronically constipated are always thinking about their discomfort, and this problem takes up much mental space. It's difficult to think of your meaning and purpose in life, when one is stuck thinking about constipation. It is even a psychological metaphor:

You are mentally stuck thinking about being physically stuck. Laxatives are a multi-million dollar industry, and constipation is a huge unspoken problem.

There is such great possibility for the improvement and alleviation of constipation through empowered nutrition. Gut and emotional health are connected. If someone is feeling, bloated, constipated, or fatigued, which can lead to depression, how will their attitude and view of life be? Many people do not know that much of our serotonin is created in the gut. Serotonin, as mentioned in the last chapter, is the "feel good hormone."

There is such a huge connection between gut health, brain health, and our mood. Functional medicine is concerned with connecting the dots, instead of keeping them all separate. Every part of our body is interrelated and affects each other. Another related problem that I see quite alarmingly in high numbers are people with gallbladder disease. I have seen many people in their 20s already having had their gallbladder removed. Why is this happening at an epidemic level? Many people also have gallstones. One likely contributing factor is all the sludge created in their gall bladders from deep-fried and hydrogenated fats, and a toxic, fast food-based, unhealthy diet, lacking in fruits, vegetables, and whole foods.

Depression and Anxiety

Serotonin, as mentioned earlier, is an inhibitory neurotransmitter associated with feeling a sense of calm, soothing, and general wellbeing when levels are sufficient. It is an important element of the complex brain chemistry picture that affects our vulnerability to depression, chronic sadness, and anxiety. In this day and age, when depression and anxiety seem to be rampant, having balanced brain chemistry is extremely important, and can help us keep a more calm and stable mood. Some symptoms of serotonin depletion are poor sleep, sugar and carbohydrate cravings, low mood, lowered immune system, low energy, irritability, and digestive problems.

Depression, in my opinion, is a bio-chemical, nutritional, emotional, and spiritual condition that needs special care. The healing process begins with a decision to change your life and enter a new journey of learning how to heal your body. It is showing you, through your symptoms, that you are depleted of necessary life-giving elements, such as a high-quality, nutritional diet. Consult with a nutritionally oriented integrative professional who can recommend a program for you that will support your healing and neurochemistry. Reach out for additional support, such as psychotherapy, support groups, massage, and other forms of healing touch. I know it can be very difficult to begin new practices when you're feeling down, so keep it simple! Taking just one step toward healing can make a big difference. Start with one new self-care practice at a time. The most important thing is that you start now. Your strength and self-esteem will grow, simply from the decision to start taking care of your self.

A few tips to consider:

1. Consider making an appointment with a psychotherapist, or an integrative doctor that specializes in depression, to explore what your options and needs are.
2. Drink more water, as a regular practice. Often people who are depressed can be dehydrated, and do not think of drinking water. It is one of the contributors to depression, and other conditions. Our brains and bodies are mostly made out of water, and we truly need to be well hydrated.
3. Start to eat healthier. Eliminate unhealthy foods, dairy, processed foods, sugar, and junk.
4. Increase life-giving, plant-based foods from nature. They will help to heal you, eaten in the right combinations. (Please see the foods to avoid and include lists in the Empowered Life Plan in Chapter

Eight.)

5. Increase your exercise. You can even begin simply by walking every day.

6. Explore other healing modalities, such as chiropractic, nutrition, massage, acupuncture, meditation, art therapy, hypnosis, tai yoga massage, spiritual books and classes that inspire you and uplift your spirit, yoga, stretching, learning to connect with your body, other mind body healing practices.

Detoxification

Detoxification is a natural, yet complex process on both the physical and biochemical level. Our liver is responsible for processing toxins, and works brilliantly if we support it with loving self-care and excellent nutrition. This metabolic and enzymatic process is constantly going on in our bodies in order to help us neutralize and detoxify chemical toxins, such as pesticides, drugs, excess alcohol, microorganisms, and chemicals in our food, water, and air. Our amazing liver filters our blood and packages toxins and fatty substances for elimination. The vast array of antioxidants and phytonutrients from whole foods are essential for our body's process of detoxification, as they aid in protecting us from the onslaught of free radicals and increased oxidative stress. When we have a powerful, balanced detoxification system, we have a much greater chance for long-term health and resilience.

Another form of detoxification is a psychological one. By separating ourselves from toxic relationships in our lives, we allow for psychological and spiritual healing, which are equally essential for our health.

Heart and Cardiovascular Health

For the prevention of heart disease, we want to have balanced blood pressure and healthy cholesterol levels. Good HDL, which is the protective cholesterol, and non-oxidized LDL, as well as low triglycerides, keeps inflammation low. Also heart-protective are healthy foods, staying and becoming lean, maintaining low insulin levels, good periodontal health, and getting consistent and moderate exercise. Keep your heart safe with lots of love and self-care, healing your heartbreak, and healing your life. Our heart is like our brain, in that we have a functional side and an emotional side, and they are both deeply connected.

Metabolic Syndrome

Metabolic syndrome is a worldwide crisis, with millions of Americans alone suffering from this. Knowing that it is preventable and reversible, I feel inspired to help people make the changes that are needed.

So what is metabolic syndrome? It is a complex set of related symptoms and risk factors such as high blood pressure, elevated blood fats along with an elevated risk of heart disease, a higher risk of stroke, excess adipose (fat) in the mid-section, obesity, elevated fasting insulin levels, low levels of HDL (the good cholesterol) and elevated, and possibly oxidized, LDL cholesterol, elevated fasting glucose which can contribute a higher risk of diabetes, elevated hemoglobin A1c, increased inflammation, polycystic ovary syndrome (PCOS), which is a hormonal imbalance in girls and women, and increased female hormones in males.

What actually happens with metabolic syndrome? All of the food that we eat, fats, proteins, and carbohydrates are broken down during digestion into proteins, micronutrients, and glucose. Our body uses the proteins and nutrients for immune function, and the repair of our cells. Glucose (sugar) is used as the body's basic fuel, which is carried through the bloodstream and put into our cells. Glucose should not be left floating in our bloodstream, however, because it has a very detrimental effect on our health if it does. Our brain and body need our blood sugar to remain stable. It is crucial to have balanced blood sugar within our body to feel our best and live preventatively. This is one of the main reasons to work towards eliminating sugar from your diet and lifestyle.

The systems of our body all want homeostasis in order to function at optimal levels for our health and wellbeing. It is the difference between having a peaceful and consistently even ride on an airplane, rather than a ride with tumultuous turbulence. Imagine the captain saying, "Stay in your seats and buckle your seatbelts. We are going through a storm, and might even have to land at a different airport!" You wouldn't want to hear that, would you?

Giving our cells the energy they need is a critical physiological function. This is the crucial role that insulin plays in our life. Insulin is a hormone that signals the liver cells, muscle cells, and fat cells, to absorb the glucose from our bloodstream. Our body's job is to regulate and adjust our blood sugar levels to what our cells demand. When working well, our body is able to release insulin in just the right amounts, which is desirable and called insulin sensitivity.

So where does the trouble come from? Our blood sugar metabolism has been greatly thrown off by our present society's very destructive excess of processed, refined, and fast food. People are ingesting high levels of sugar, which is causing damage in our cells. When sugar quickly enters the bloodstream, our body has to release high levels of insulin in order to keep the excessive amount of glucose from being poured into the bloodstream and damaging our cells. If this keeps happening repeatedly, our cells become tired, working so hard to protect us against harm, and they can become compromised. They start becoming insensitive to our body's signaling system, which knows when our blood sugar is too high, and needs an immediate response from our insulin. We become insulin-resistant when we become insulin insensitive, and this sets into motion many other negative metabolic consequences.

When we become insulin resistant, we often feel fatigued, experience constant hunger, and gain weight. One of the symptoms that make people most unhappy is the excess fat all around their middle. Our body was not made to sustain constant high levels of insulin to try to manage all the excess sugar that is being ingested. This process is what damages our cellular metabolism, and pushes us toward a greater risk for diabetes, heart disease, depression, and high levels of inflammation.

But this is a whole body problem, not just a sugar problem. All of these risks and symptoms affect each other, and the further along we are on this destructive continuum, the higher our risk is of developing everything we do not want.

So What Are the Solutions?

Loving Self-Care, Healing Stress

Taking loving care of ourselves is crucial, as it has many far-reaching effects, such as relieving chronic stress, disharmony, and inner conflict. This is often where our work begins. We often neglect our health and nutritional needs when we are under stress, which can lead to self-punishing attitudes and behaviors.

What are some solutions to this pattern, and how do we deal with the intense need to be satisfied? We must find a way to still have pleasure in our food, and still eat healthfully and in a way that honors our body. One solution is to become proactive in creating dishes that are wonderful and satisfying, and have excellent ingredients that do not cause havoc in our bodies. In other words, we should stop viewing ourselves as on a diet, but rather find ourselves blessed to have found a nutritional lifestyle that we live, love, and embrace.

As we look together at the deeper domain of our nutritional struggles that live within us, the question arises again: Why are our struggles so universal? Often when people are struggling with their physical health and striving to follow a seemingly impossible nutritional game plan, they feel isolated and alone. But the good news is that you are not alone! Isn't it comforting to know that this is a very human and universal problem? The struggle aspect of wellness emanates from our confused and critical mind, rather than as a compassionate, intuitive, aligned connection to our selves. How did we lose this primal connection to the real health needs of our bodies, minds, and spirits?

We Have a Choice!

Why would we deny our bodies the fuel that is provided by the brilliance of nature, in a way that makes us feel truly well, and would support us on a cellular level? Why is self-care such a struggle for so many? It can be deeply empowering to realize that the freedom to honor our bodies by eating consciously and lovingly, rather than eating in a way that increases our suffering, is possible.

We need to eat more mindfully, both for our health and for our general compassion for ourselves. We need a food and lifestyle reboot in our lives. We need to find the inner peace that can only come about by becoming in balance with ourselves. Our society has replaced healthy whole foods like fruits, the vast variety of vegetables, fresh herbs and spices, deep greens, sprouts, sea vegetables, seeds, nuts, nut butters, berries, avocados, beans, clean non-toxic proteins, organic gluten-free grains, like millet, quinoa, and brown rice, with fast and processed foods; devastatingly unhealthy "food," which is having a destructive and treacherous effect on human health.

Right now, today, we have the opportunity to transform! The time is now; let the paradigm shift begin!

MSG and Artificial Sweeteners

The first powerfully helpful move toward wellness would be to immediately eliminate all artificial sweeteners, like saccharin, aspartame, maltose, maltodextrin, sucralose, asuflame, and saccharine, which are neurotoxins, out of your diet. A very brilliant neurosurgeon, Dr. Russell Blaylock, wrote the book, *Excitoxins: The Taste That Kills.* He brought to light the dangers of glutamate and the intensely harmful effects it can have on our health. He cited the most harmful excititoxins to avoid, which are MSG, aspartame, caseinate (often used in baby and toddler foods), hydrolyzed protein, and yeast extract. These substances are used by the food industry, and are not only totally unnecessary, but they are very harmful to the body.[6]

There are numerous glutamate receptors in the body, and the bottom line is that when you consume MSG, or its derivatives called by more benign-sounding names, our level of glutamate in the blood can increase many fold. Stimulated glutamate receptors can contribute to irritable bowel, reflux, headaches (including migraine headaches), and even heart attacks, because of the cardiac receptors. Elevated glutamate levels can also possibly increase our risk of degenerative brain illnesses such as Parkinson's and Alzheimer's Diseases. High glutamate levels also increase our risk of cancer. When our magnesium levels are low, our glutamate receptors can become hypersensitive. Athletes are at increased risk when, right before exercise, they have a meal with MSG or a Diet Coke™ with aspartame, which can cause intense cardiac irritability.

Artificial sweeteners are greatly acidic and detrimental to our whole body and brain. They are also known to keep us craving sugar. Some nutrients that help to block glutamate in the body are curcumin, flavonoids, silimarin, and ginkgo biloba. There are approximately forty names for MSG. For more information on MSG, please check Dr. Blaylock's website, at www.blaylockreport.com. If we eat whole foods that are unprocessed,

---

[6]Blaylock, Russell. *Excitoxins: The Taste That Kills.* Santa Fe: Health Press, 1997.

we greatly lessen our contact with these troubling ingredients.

GMOs

Genetically modified organisms, or GMOs, are everywhere, and it's important for everyone to be informed about them. Companies, using chemical processes and numerous pesticides, are genetically altering original, precious seeds from nature. These are seeds that all of our produce, grains, and plants are made from. GMOs are affecting our food supply, and they present a great risk to our families' health, affecting all generations to come.

GMOs were first introduced in the mid 1990s. According to Jeffrey Smith, a leading expert on the dangers of GMOS, "Organisms that are a result of a laboratory process where genes from the DNA of one species are extracted and artificially forced into the genes of an unrelated plant or animal. These foreign genes may come from bacteria, viruses, insects, animals, or even humans."[7] There are numerous chemical and toxic pesticides and herbicides involved with the GMO process, which are terribly concerning for our health and our planet. I highly recommend an award-winning documentary by Jeffery Smith called *Genetic Roulette*, to learn more about this subject. On his websites (www.responsible technology.org and www.geneticroulettemovie.com) he provides a non-GMO shopping list and other essential information.

GMOs are present in the majority of our fresh and processed foods in the US, even though they are banned in a number of countries in Europe and other places in the world. Presently in our country, it is not required to label which products have GMO ingredients. This is deeply concerning.

Crops that are GMOs (unless organically sourced, and certified non-GMO):
• Alfalfa

---

[7]Jeffery Smith, www.responsibletechnology.org.

- Corn, polenta, corn oil, corn chips, and all corn products that are put into so many food products
- Canola
- Soy, soybean oil, soy sauce, and all soy products
- Cotton, cottonseed oil, and cottonseed products
- Sugar beets
- Certain crops of zucchini and squash
- Hawaiian papaya

This is a growing list, so please stay updated with this information through www.responsibletechnology.org and other organizations that provide this essential information.

Tips to avoid GMOs:
- Eat as organic as possible
- Know the GMO crops, and avoid them and their ingredients
- Eat plant-based as much as possible
- Avoid factory farmed meat, fish, and eggs. In factory farming the animals are treated extremely poorly. They are often fed GMO products which negatively affect their health and that of those who choose to consume them. There is also extensive information available on the destructive effects of factory farming on the environment.
- Avoid dairy. Cows are injected with hormones that have very worrying health effects and risks, and on top of that, they are also GMOs!
- Avoid all processed food, deep-fried food, and fast food. They often have many GMO ingredients.
- Be careful when going into restaurants. Ask what kind of oil they use in their dishes. Avoid all corn oil, canola oil, vegetable oil, cottonseed oil, and soybean oil. Not only are they poor quality oils, but they are also usually GMO.

- If eating soy products like tofu, tempeh, or miso, look for only non-GMO products
- Other ingredients that may be GMO: soy lecithin, soy protein, cornstarch, high fructose corn syrup, aspartame, and various other artificial sweeteners.

Sugar, Processed Food, and Weight Loss

Eliminating sugar is one of the most crucial and health protective actions we can take. I have seen numerous patients have a totally different experience when sugar is in their body, and when it is not. When their body is free from sugar, their cravings stop and their hunger is diminished. Eating sugar causes our bodies to call forth insulin, which has been referred to as the hunger and storage hormone. It creates excess adipose (fat) around our midsection, which truly makes people miserable and frustrated. Many people come to my office and ask me how they got this excess fat around their middle, sometimes looking like they have a tire circling their waistline. This is a metabolic response to the storage of excess fat that sugar creates in our bodies. Sugar also creates emotional irritability and fatigue. It contributes to increased inflammation, gut fermentation, mood swings, poor sleep, cravings, and increased addiction. It's hard for many people to picture being able to eliminate sugar, when they feel so addicted to it and consistently have it in their bodies.

One of the amazingly satisfying things I do in my practice is to assist people in breaking their sugar addiction. They begin to experience their taste buds changing, and they eventually lose their cravings for sugar and processed foods all together. They then have greater energy and often report a tremendous improvement in their blood tests. It is true that going off sugar and processed foods, and eating in a healthier whole food way with moderate exercise, can dramatically reduce belly fat. It is an exhilarating, health enhancing, and extremely liberating experience to burn fat instead of store it.

Reducing and Preventing Inflammation

Studies show that people who are very stressed, both from poor nutrition, and those who live in chronic emotional stress states, have higher levels of inflammation, oxidative stress, and increased vulnerability to illness. Excess oxidation in the brain and body is like a rusting process. It accelerates aging, and it creates excess and systemic inflammation in the body. When inflammation begins, it goes everywhere. It's like the beginning of a forest fire that spreads over many acres, destroying beautiful forests in its path, until it is finally put out!

Increased inflammation and oxidative stress show up as cataracts, wrinkles, age spots, cancer, inflammatory conditions, cardiovascular disease, autoimmune conditions, and can damage our neuronal cells. Accelerated oxidative stress can damage our DNA, and can play a role in all degenerative diseases.

Another positive step is to eliminate deep-fried food, which are so plentiful in restaurants and fast food establishments, and are often cooked in poor quality, highly processed, unhealthy oils, continually frying and re-frying the foods, which increases oxidative stress, free radicals, and trans fats in our bodies. Even at home, heating oils to a very high level can be highly detrimental to our health. Frying changes the oil into a very unhealthy chemical disaster. Fried foods contribute to obesity and an increase of inflammation, which is the beginning point of all chronic illnesses.

Processed foods are also de-natured and empty of the nutrients our bodies truly need and depend on for wellness. To lower and prevent inflammation, we need nine to thirteen servings of vegetables and lower glycemic fruits and berries, with a much greater emphasis on deep greens.

Food for Thought:
9 to 13 servings of vegetables and low-glycemic fruits per day,
lowers and prevents inflammation!

Nature provides thousands of phytonutrients and antioxidants from the vast array of beautiful plant foods available to us. Our bodies truly need these on a cellular level. They help to lower inflammation, add alkalinity, and are protective to our immune system in so many essential ways for our health. Fresh produce is also essential to eat every day.

Healthy vs. Unhealthy Oils

One huge health mistake many people make, is to use unhealthy oils. Oils to avoid are vegetable, corn, cottonseed, safflower, sunflower, canola, and soybean, plus hydrogenated fats. The best way to include fats in your diet is through whole food, plant-based fats, such as avocados, raw nuts, seeds, nut butters, tahini, olives, flax seeds, chia seeds, and hemp seeds in small amounts. Many people use way too much oil, and often it's the processed, unhealthy, pro-inflammatory ones.

Eliminate Dairy Foods - Eliminate Congestion

Dairy causes congestion in our bodies, which then drains through our organs. Many people suffer sinus infections, upper respiratory and bronchial illnesses, post-nasal drip, asthma, and ear infections that are exacerbated by the congestion and toxic load that dairy foods create. Dairy from factory farming often contains steroid hormones that are also GMOs, and antibiotics that are given to cows in order to make them grow faster and continually produce more and more milk. These substances have potent destructive effects on our bodies, and are very worrisome for human health. The artificial hormones, pesticides, and antibiotics that are given to these poor animals, complicate the harm of ingesting their dairy excretions even further. Many young children and babies react to dairy foods by having reoccurring ear infections, and in treatment, are given antibiotics, which eliminates the healthy flora from their digestive tract. This then has further consequences for their gut, their immune system, and their overall health. More and more rounds of antibiotics are prescribed, but they rarely have had it suggested to them to go off dairy completely, which is a non-invasive, and often a simple, life changing solution.

I have seen so many patient's lives and health improve by removing dairy from their diets. Creaminess offers a very attractive texture for many people, and they don't realize that there are alternatives. Non-dairy items can create delicious foods from ice cream, to sauces, to puddings, soups, and salad dressings. I can tell you, it feels great to go through a whole year with no colds or congestion! If you are congested, this is your body telling you that dairy does not agree with you. **Our bodies speak to us in our symptoms.**

Another important aspect is the dairy protein called casein. Ingesting casein can contribute to the risk of cancer, which is studied closely in *The China Study* by Dr. Colin Campbell.[8] There is also more information on this from Dr. Neil Barnard at his website, the Physicians Committee for Responsible Medicine: www.pcrm.org, and well as many more references as to why dairy and casein are not good for us.

If we look back to nature, all animals drink their mother's milk until weaning. They do not go and start drinking the milk of another species, whose milk was designed for those colts, calves, kittens, or baby elephants. It is entirely possible to enjoy a healthy life of not eating dairy.

We have been brainwashed to think that creamy means dairy, and many people are attached and even addicted to it. There is so much information written about why dairy can be addictive. It is because of the

---

[8]Campbell, Colin. *The China Study*. BenBella Books: Dallas, 2004.

opiate effect that the chemical breakdown of casein, the dairy protein, into casomorphins has on our digestion process. There are many non-dairy ways to create a creamy consistency. We can use almond cream or coconut cream, and there are also many delicious cheeses made from seeds and nuts, and other wonderful ingredients.

It is an addictive cycle. As we are triggered biochemically by sugar, dairy, and junk food, our hunger increases for even more junk food and sugar, white flour, fast foods, processed foods, high fructose corn syrup, corn syrup, deep fried foods, artificial sweeteners, genetically modified foods, factory farmed animal foods, excessive caffeine, and alcohol. When people eat this way their minds can becomes fuzzy, and they often feel tired, bloated, depressed, teary, irritable, and isolated. We experience a sense of "false hunger," which greatly misleads us and disconnects us from our body's true needs. When we see ourselves once again trapped in this vicious cycle, it also hurts our self-esteem and our sense of self. This state of biochemical imbalance disconnects us from our true self and prevents us from realizing our higher potential. Prolonged psychological and biochemical changes can occur, and we are greatly imposing stress on our entire body and brain to overcome the detrimental effects of these substances.

A common symptom of eating these foods is a constant craving for more junk, so we are tricked into thinking and believing that we can't do without them. It's like trying to convince an alcoholic why they should stop drinking while they are already drunk. Eating this way can also raise our anxiety, increase depression, and push us into adrenal fight or flight response, which leads to fatigue, creates immune system suppression, brain fog, gut dis-regulation and gut fermentation, inflammation, reflux, constipation, and irritable bowel.

Our deeper wisdom and developing intuition are waiting for us to shine our light on them through our wellness and our desire to feel love and be loved. Being in a state of love creates great feel-good endorphins, and great brain and body chemicals. If we are thrown off-course, we can lose our way, manifesting in not feeling well because of a disconnect from our true selves. This disconnect then mixes up with our biochemistry and we become confused and often addicted to perceived relief by eating more junk, at the expense of our health.

Having a true connection with our inspired path is the best prescription needed for our health. Picture going to a doctor and receiving this written prescription:

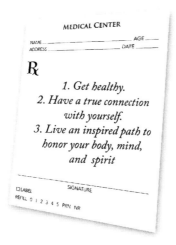

Perhaps why so many people are struggling with their mind and body in conflict, is because they are looking for a diet, when what they really need is deep connection with themselves for true and lasting success. Being aligned is not being in battle with oneself. It is not about will power and control. It is about surrendering and melting our resistances for a higher cause, becoming one with our self; to rise above the mundane fight with ourselves and our unsatisfying desires, and finding real love, peace, and freedom within. Our fear of deprivation at the thought of separating ourselves from our familiar, unhealthy foods, is really a cover for the true longing for our inner wholeness. There is no taste or material object that can replace the true connection with our heart, mind, and body. How many people do you know that have so much in their lives, but still feel so empty inside? Why is there so much depression and anxiety in so many people? What are we really missing? Why do we keep looking in places where we don't find what we need, but instead find more frustration and more emptiness?

What is amazing is that if you get this, and connect to this passage right now, your life can change! It is the recognition that you are longing to find the real you, the YOU that is there under all the layers of all that has occurred in your life, needing to be seen and loved by you.

Cancer and Nutrition

Cancer is a very complex subject, however there is much we can do towards prevention, even after having gone through it. I feel deep compassion for anyone who has, or is facing, this challenge. One important factor in your battle is your attitude about it. Do not let cancer become your identity. You are still who you are in your heart. It is crucial to find the sources of hope, healing, and inspiration in your mind and in your spirit, no matter what.

Please consider avoiding dairy, meat, and all junk, fast, and processed food. Become plant-based with vital, living, healing foods. It is also best to avoid nitrates, factory-farmed meats and fish, GMOs, deep-fried food, hydrogenated and trans fats, sugar, corn syrup, high fructose corn syrup, and soda.

From the *Textbook of Functional Medicine*, "Researchers have recently discovered that specific nutrients modify the expression and function of detoxification genes. Cruciferous vegetables, which include broccoli, cauliflower, Brussels sprouts, and cabbage, contain nutrients called glucosinolates."[9] These are protective substances that can aid our immune system and our prevention processes.

This is part of the reason why all of the major institutions around the world that are concerned with health, recommend high levels of fruits and vegetables everyday. There are integrative oncologists who you can give you a comprehensive program that includes nutritional guidance.

Greater Alkalinity/Less Acidity in Your Diet

It is important to avoid processed food because it acidifies the body, and makes us more vulnerable to illness. Whole food, plant-based, abundant vegetables, especially lots of deep greens, will improve alkalinity in the body, which is incredibly protective. Drinking naturally pure water is essential. Always check, when possible, the pH levels of the water you drink when buying bottled water. You can find listings online of the pH of bottled water. Avoid all sodas, especially diet soda, because of high acidity, and either high fructose corn syrup, saccharin, sucralose, or aspartame, which are all highly toxic and acid-forming.

Healthy Vital Aging

Healthy aging is the ability to claim and utilize the power of nutrition, prevention practices, and finding our meaning and purpose in life. It can

---

[9]Jones, David, et al. "Healthy Aging: the Promotion of Organ Reserve." *Textbook for Functional Medicine*. The Institute for Functional Medicine: Gig Harbor, WA, 2006

help us to create the vitality to live out all our years in better health. There are many preventive self-care practices that can be implemented to achieve our greatest potential in healthy aging.

Don't Think Your Way into New Behavior, Behave Your Way into New Thinking

To begin really integrating true self-care is the next step in improving our biochemistry. For many people, learning self-care is a challenge. After spending so much of their lives putting themselves last, it is an odd concept to love, plan, and care for one's self. I feel deeply that this is a missing element when people decide to go on the next diet, without connecting to the part of them that needs self-care and self-respect. We need a comprehensive life program that we can deeply internalize, instead of a superimposed diet plan that we don't really own for ourselves. Connecting with this part of ourselves can provide so much wisdom that comes from within. By finding the part of us that can grow, we begin to enliven, but if we do not tune into this part of us, we just stay in a rigid thinking pattern that keeps us stuck.

There are some crucial steps we can take towards improving our biochemistry through emotional growth and behavioral change:

Positive defiance (A term coined by Dr. Viktor Frankl). Defiance is not always negative. At times we need to positively defy negative influences and thoughts, and embrace what is positive. To become empowered, listen to your deepest intuition, get in touch with your truth, and become educated and informed through awareness. We need to determine what does not feel right for us and, with love and respect, find our own truth and make crucial decisions and empowered choices for our lives.

Keep your adrenals healthy! Stop multitasking all the time, and meditate, find fun ways to move regularly, have fun, lower or eliminate caffeine, have a healthy diet, and make sure you get a good night's sleep. Your adrenals are adorable and powerful organs sitting right on top of your kidneys, and they regulate many crucial hormones in your body, especially how you adapt to stress. They decide, "Are we going to be resilient or burnt out?" How we treat our body, affects the health of our adrenals, how we overcome stress, and hence, our entire experience of life.

Never Stop Learning. Having a healthy, meaningful life is about learning, healing, and making progress in your life. This is perhaps why people lose interest or fall off the wagon, even when they are doing well for a while. They make strong, powerful changes, but then they revert back to their more destructive patterns in the end. This process does not work as an intellectual exercise. It's like being stuck in your head and forgetting that you have a body to take care of, with a real beating heart and true needs.

Seek and Provide Emotional Support and Community. There is a psychoneuroimmun-ological connection between our endocrine system, our brain, and our entire body. Studies show how crucial emotional support, connection to community, experiencing love, and having a spiritual connection to life, is in keeping us in a vital state of health. These essential connections help us be more resilient to stressors. Finding and having meaning and purpose in our lives is an incredibly important aspect of health that is not focused on enough in our society, yet is a crucial part of the healing process. I feel strongly that on medical forms there should be questions like,

"Do you feel isolated?
"Do you feel connected to a community?"
"Do you have good friends?"
"Do you feel highly regarded and respected?"

"Do you feel meaning and purpose in your life?"
"How are your most significant relationships?"

We don't really know what people are going through, until we truly know. Many people are privately going through very difficult times, and that important information won't be uncovered if we, or a doctor, don't invite them to talk about who they really are. This brings to mind Dr. Bernie Siegel's work, in which he describes his own depression as a surgeon because he was simply operating on people without knowing who they really were and the life challenges they've had. When he started asking these questions of his patients, everything changed, including better outcomes for their immune system. It makes a huge difference in our health on all levels when we feel cared about, and we begin caring about ourselves. This important concept leads back to the integral need in our society for greater empathy and compassion.

*****

A truly holistic and integrative way is needed to see the whole person, to help them heal what they need to, and to meet them wherever they are in the process. My approach is functional medicine based, which investigates and understands the underlying cause, no matter what aspect of their being needs care.

Health is precious and a great blessing. Our health is profoundly affected by our thoughts, feelings, beliefs about ourselves, and our nutritional wellness practices. With empowered nutrition there is so much we can do about our wellbeing. Whatever our challenges are, we can apply nutritional intervention, psychological healing, and the choice of a philosophy and attitude that guide us from the wisdom within and set the stage for healing. Are we willing to embrace the changes that set us free? The freedom to become who we truly are, and to realize our best potential, should always be our goal.

The Spirituality of Wellness

Chapter Five

"While we have the gift of life, it seems to me the only
tragedy is to allow part of us to die – whether it is our
spirit, our creativity or our glorious uniqueness."
—Gilda Radner

The spirituality of wellness refers to our philosophy of life. Do you know your philosophy of life? I recommend that you take a little time, and free-write on paper what you believe about life. It is the spiritual blueprint that you live by, and it influences you in every way. Then write your spiritual beliefs about your wellness, what you have been through, and what is possible now for your wellbeing.

Spirituality has always been very important to me, even before I knew what it was. It first came to me as a feeling and a longing without having the words for it. I remember thinking as a young girl that "there has to be more to all of it than this." I am so deeply happy and grateful to say that I now know within myself that there is more to it all, and though it is an ongoing, unfolding education, it is indeed quite amazing. We are connected with experiences and people that touch us in such depth-full ways. There are the difficult Zen masters in our lives, who just by being themselves, push our buttons and stir up our deepest stuff. They provide the means for us to look at, learn from, and grow into a deeper understanding of ourselves, and what is happening in our world. We can kick and scream all we want, and then we can grow.

When our hearts get broken, our spiritual process can help us to open a new door of insight, wisdom, and love. This chapter is about replacing fear with hope and possibility; it is an internal transformation in order to become more of who you truly are. Wellness encompasses much more than how and what we eat, and the nutrients we take, or our childhood wounds and defense mechanisms.

Hurting: A Window into Self-Understanding

Sometimes what we have to face is deeply painful, shocking, and heartbreaking. Many people go through very difficult periods, which are often referred to metaphorically as the "dark night of the soul." Multiple crises happen at once, and we wonder how we will possibly get through. One of the most universal things people say to me when in my office is, "Something happened in my life that I never thought I would ever be going through." As we struggle to grow and resolve our challenges and difficulties, new ones continually pop up with various dimensions to them.

By allowing ourselves to grieve for our own pain, we can learn and deepen our compassion and empathy for, not only ourselves, but for all suffering beings. We can create something in the world that brings comfort and healing to others. Dr. Viktor Frankl said that the remedy for profound loss is to find meaning and purpose in our lives. There is such a powerful need for the human spirit to overcome adversity. Consistently, I see people suffering when they haven't yet identified their meaning and purpose in life; however finding our purpose is always available to us if we know to start looking. When facing adversity, there is always outer and inner help available.

People often need encouragement and support to be reminded that they have a greater purpose, and that their life has meaning. Tapping into our deeper wisdom is essential to our ongoing wellness. Life has both joy and sadness in it. It is an innate longing of our heart and soul to know how we make a difference in this world, and that we are important to someone.

The world needs you, and the essence that you bring, to contribute in some way to the huge needs that exist. Giving to others makes a difference in their lives, as well as fills our own spirit. It is then written in the Book of Life forever.

By sharing a deep and satisfying connection with others, and enriching our intuition, we expand our capacity to love and be loved. By facing our fears of intimacy, we can create real connection and communion with others. By using tenderness, love, and honor, we can take our brush and paint the world with love. You are capable of touching spiritual delight, and when you do, you will never be the same again. You are greater than you ever thought. Life can mirror to us a reflection of what we are truly capable of, and it'll blow your mind in the best way possible. In searching for our potential for greater wellness, we may stumble upon a deep well within us filled with beauty, love, and wisdom. Dip into it! You'll find the meaning and purpose of self-care, beautiful nutrition, kindness, and self-respect. It can bring about the beginning of a new life of deeper satisfaction, goodness, and fulfillment. This is why spiritual wellness is so crucial to our health; we need to take care of ourselves with love.

When we have a health challenge, or a diagnosis we did not want or expect, what are we going to do with this spiritually? This is a crucial question, because it will influence how things unfold for you, no matter what you, a doctor, or others might project. How you perceive it psychologically and spiritually makes all the difference in how your journey will be. When we change our attitude toward a condition we are dealing with, it can change our experience of that situation, no matter what we are facing.

The Soul

Know that you have a soul, and that every cell within you has divine energy within it. We can affect our cells through the love and messages we have circulating through our being. We can enliven our cells, our wellness, and our energy simply by opening our heart and soul to our journey with integrity.

Here are some signs of your aliveness of soul and spirit:

1. ***Being creative, curious, playful, and imaginative.***

    Exploring music, art, dance, singing, and divine music. Isn't this what we love about children? We need to awaken and enliven these qualities in us again.

2. ***The ability to open your heart to give and receive love.***

    Keeping yourself open to love, even if past wounds urge you to close yourself off. There are the fears of change and rejection, that can cloud our spirituality, and which can result in the symptoms of feeling disconnected and separate, which in truth we are not.

3. ***The ability to cultivate compassion and empathy for ourselves, and others.***

    We never know what others are going through, until we deeply know their story, their heartbreak, their losses, and their resilience. Finding creative ways to express the compassion and care that is needed, will touch others. Simply by meeting us, we've made a difference in their lives, just as others have done for us. Who has touched you deeply in your life? What did you learn from them that made a great difference to you?

We can learn to treat our body and soul with love. By eating healthier to honor your body, breathing deeply, and beginning some regular movement, such as exercise, yoga, and stretching, you can treat yourself with more love. Setting healthy boundaries, facing something you are afraid to deal with, and finding support and a safe space can help with what you are carrying around in your heart.

We can also simply notice the meaningful and repetitive themes in our life, and look at them as tools, rather than obstacles. How we hold what happens to us makes all the difference in our level of wellness. By having a deep spiritual commitment to finding the meaning and purpose in your life, you can have a strong foundation with which to weather the storms of life. This message has been embedded in my soul from the teachings of Viktor Frankl and the Viktor Frankl Institute for Meaning-Centered Therapy, a graduate institute I attended.

> *Paradox Box:*
> The more we look within, the
> more we can see without.

If your vessel is tired, it's hard to hear the very important life messages arising for you out of deeper wisdom, inspiring more clarity and helping us to tune into our own intuition for knowledge and guidance. Often when people are living in a self-sabotaging way, and not feeling well as a result, they become distracted and can miss the jewels and juiciness of life. They are unable to see the wisdom waiting for them, and the deeper satisfaction available.

We often need something inspiring to come into our presence and remind us of the real light we have within that guides our way, even if we are dealing with hardship in our lives. When these special moments of inspiration arrive, they can seem like coincidences. Perhaps there is a deeper synchronicity to life than we realize; a force that is anonymous and there to help us. How many of these moments have we really had and not noticed? Perhaps it was someone who off-handedly said something that made all the difference, or helped us in a profound way we will never forget.

"Synchronicity is the coming together of inner and outer events in a way that cannot be explained by cause and effect and is meaningful to the observer."
—Carl Jung

Even with the bittersweet nature of life, with all the joys and the sorrows, the most powerful force in the universe is love. The voice of our higher self, our intuition, comes alive and speaks to us through insight. We are mind, body, and spirit, and all aspects affect each other continuously.

To gain a foothold in a spiritual self-care practice, we need to cultivate:

1. **Attitude**

   Whatever we approach in life, our attitude towards it will have a huge impact of how we go through it and how we experience it, and what we ultimately do with it.

2. **Discipline**

   By learning to be consistent with your life's plan, and becoming grounded in long-term satisfaction and success, instead of impulsive, short-term false satisfaction, can save you from derailment and regret. You can make new habits, as it only takes time for new habits to form.

3. **Learning to keep your word to yourself**

   Become someone you can trust, follow through with your promises to yourself, and keep your word no matter what. This is actually a very settling and non-conflicting way to live, and it keeps your focus and passion on creating what you want.

4. **Living in integrity**

   As you let go of self-doubt and unworthiness, you gain self-esteem, self-respect, and gain confidence in yourself and your choices.

In the sacred texts from nearly all of the cultures and religions of the world, there are beautiful passages about honoring our body, taking care of our health, and treating our body as a gift to love and respect. I often turn to these quotes for inspiration:

"The eye is the lamp of the body.
So, if your eye is healthy, your whole body will be full of light."
—*Matthew* 6:22

"Once I knew only darkness and stillness...my life was without past or future...but a little word from the fingers of another fell into my hand that clutched at emptiness, and my heart leaped to the rapture of living."
—Helen Keller

"As far as we can discern, the sole purpose of human existence is to kindle a light in the darkness of mere being."
—Carl Jung

New positive changes and behaviors can have a most amazing positive effect on us. If we are feeling down and consumed with beating ourselves up, we can miss many opportunities for friendships, love relationships, jobs, and seeing and realizing our true potential. We need our own positive energy and wisdom to guide and strengthen us. Life is like a flowing river, always changing and bringing us toward places unknown.

By creating an invisible realm within, where you can restore, repair, and become inspired, where your creativity can flow and your wisdom reign, a place more real than the illusion of the world, seeds can be planted that will manifest with delight. In this place, your actions begin to compliment what is in truth for you, and your being and your cells flow towards healing, peace, resilience, no matter what is experienced.

We become heroes in our own lives by honoring our own health, dignity, heart, and soul, while we honor the health, dignity, heart, and soul of others. This makes our lives truly rich with meaning. Often people feel lonely no matter how many people are around, or what material possessions they have. It is an aspect of emptiness, which only rich meaning can satisfy and help us to be more enlivened. They are outwardly focused, and often a very human trap is to think, "If I only had this, then my life would be so much better." However, as soon as we get whatever "this" is, it ends up being totally different than we projected and imagined, and often brings with it a whole new set of challenges, joys, disappointments, and problems. If there is someone who feels alone, and believes that no one cares about them, when this person comes to realize that there are others who do actually care for them, and that they are indeed all right, it can save a soul, even a life. Honoring someone's existence saves the world one person at a time. It is a gift to us to be fortunate enough to help others, as we are integral members of the world.

There is something called the "wellness of giving." It is something that I realized is ingrained into the very fiber of our being, and it occurs when we help someone. We come to find that it truly makes us feel good.

Further, there is research that when we help someone, it literally helps our wellness and physiology in very specific ways, such as lowering our blood pressure, creating feel good endorphins, relieving depression, and strengthening our immune system and our spirit. This is nature's way of rewarding us for doing good deeds. It is not the reason we do it, it is what happens physiologically, spiritually, and emotionally, when we create goodness, generosity, love, and help for others.

As we age, we can still be vital and creative, and continue to grow in spirituality and wisdom. In many of the cultures of the world, the elders were the ones who the younger generations came to for guidance and support. As we embrace healthy aging, we can become the loving sages that we have the potential to be. Part of this process is claiming our own love, freedom, and wellness. We can treat each day as precious, and be grateful for the opportunity to be vital, loving, and able to give back to a world that needs our help. What you believe is essential: your mind set, the lens you look through, the images of aging that you personally have and project onto yourself. Do we picture vitality, energy, and health?

By finding the fountain of wellness within, you allow your spirituality to flow like a beautiful stream of pure flowing water in a brook, meandering through a forest of majestic trees and nature's beauty. It is depth-full, beautiful, and wisdom-filled.

So what do the stages of Spiritual Wellness look like?

Stage 1

We begin to open our awareness to greater realizations, expanding our emotional, nutritional, and spiritual horizons in an ongoing process.

Stage 2

The beginning of sage-making. We gain deeper insights and compassion and use them wisely in our own lives.

Stage 3

By healing our psychology, we open the door to our spirituality. We are able to bring a greater integration of all the aspects of our self into a practice for everyday living; our psychology, our nutritional lifestyle, and our spiritual reservoir, all create a positive cycle which enrich each other.

Stage 4

We become a healing and calming presence, bringing light and wisdom not only to our own life, but to others'. We become a wise and effective mentor and leader.

Facing Darkness/Moving Towards Light

"People are like stained glass windows. They sparkle
and shine when the sun is out, but when the
darkness sets in, their true beauty is revealed
only if there is a light from within."
—Elisabeth Kubler Ross

Being human can certainly be challenging, as everyone has difficulties, heartbreaks, losses, and something to heal. Things happen to us that we never thought we would be dealing with, and we find ourselves in a position where we need to rally our spirit, our mind, and our body, to find a way through the darkness and into the light. As we face our challenges, we can set our spirit in the direction of growth, by learning new wisdom from our adversity, and creating a plan for how we will deal with the issues in the most constructive way possible.

Carl Jung once said, "There is no coming to consciousness without pain. People will do anything, no matter how absurd, in order to avoid facing their own soul. One does not become enlightened by imagining figures of light, but by making the darkness conscious."[10] I think this a crucial point, because I believe that we can prevent so much suffering if we

---

[10]Jung, Carl. Psychological Reflections: *An Anthology of the Writings of C. G. Jung*. Michigan: Harper, 1961.

can clearly see which choices we have which can lead to destructiveness and darkness, and which ones can lead to safety and light. There are some decisions that people make that they truly regret for the rest of their lives. We can only, then, make amends, learn from our mistakes, and truly change what we need to in ourselves. Difficult situations bring us closer to facing ourselves, as we deal with painful emotions, and try to navigate through our hardships. It is doubly hard if we believed that we would rarely have to deal with any difficulties in our lives. This becomes quite an eye-opener when something difficult does happen that we did not expect, even if it was our own actions that created the trouble.

There are so many inspiring stories of human beings overcoming adversity of all kinds who were also healed through the vehicle of helping others. It is helpful to embrace this truth, so that we can consider what healing we need, and how to help others in the process. It is by embracing the darkness of our lives that we can begin to heal it and then move into the light of wisdom and awareness.

Connecting Love, Freedom, and Wellness

Chapter Six

"Love is the only way to grasp another human being in the
innermost core of his personality. No one can become fully aware
of the very essence of another human being unless he loves him.
By his love he is enabled to see the essential traits and features in
the beloved person; and even more, he sees that which is potential
in him, which is not yet actualized but yet ought to be actualized.
Furthermore, by his love, the loving person enables the beloved
person to actualize these potentialities. By making him
aware of what he can be and of what he should become,
he makes these potentialities come true."
—Viktor E. Frankl, *Man's Search for Meaning*

When we have balanced wellness in our lives, it can be such a joy and
a gift to be alive. When you connect freedom with love and wellness you
have a powerful synergy, like creating a real life humble superhero with
special human powers. These are the real superpowers we are all capable
of having when we develop these aspects of ourselves. But do we choose
to see the transformation that is possible in ourselves, and our own lives,
and invest our energy, heart, and soul into our own evolution? That is the
question.

An Empowered Life

This is what balanced Love, Freedom, and Wellness looks like:

Feeling energized

Excellent digestion and detoxification

A strong balanced immune system

Good sleep

A flat belly

Healthy weight for our height and frame

Healthy lean muscle

Healthy blood pressure and vessels

A healthy heart, pancreas, and liver

Low inflammation

High levels of antioxidants

Balanced nutrition

A healthy brain and flowing neurotransmitters in balance

Feeling creative

Being humorous

Having resilience

Having a positive attitude

Having a sharp memory

Gaining ongoing knowledge of who we are

Ongoing and developing greater wisdom and inner knowing

Feeling vital and sexy and wise at every age

Feeling love

Being and exuding love to all we meet

Participating in small and big acts of generosity and kindness

Extending love wherever we can

Healing ourselves with love, understanding, and compassion for all
the adversity we have been through

We find meaning, purpose, and the legacy of our life

We are compassionate towards others, whether we understand their
pain or not

The process of integrating love, freedom, and wellness connects us to our authentic journey in this life. By realizing the ways in which we will make a difference in the world, we can begin to fill our hearts with meaning instead of emptiness. This process helps us to gently wake up to the importance of finding our true path of freedom and inspiration, in order to become who we truly are.

This is often the missing piece. We can have so much in our lives and still be missing ourselves. That untapped part of us gnaws at us from the inside, sometimes causing us to look in the wrong places in order to fill our emptiness. We have an inner longing to be fulfilled, and this pull of the spirit won't be quiet no matter what we do to numb it out. It might feel uncomfortable to feel unfulfilled, and we might have guilt for not being grateful enough for all we have, but unless we meet this exquisite human need to make a positive difference, something will be missing.

Our wellness becomes our platform for realizing our true potential of physical, mental, and spiritual health. If we are brave, and face what needs to be faced within, we are able to bring our newfound love out into the world. It has more meaning, power, and lasting effect if we first claim it for ourselves, and than manifest our powerful energy to help others. The gifts that can come from this are greater than we can imagine. Whatever your journey of courage may be, your willingness to change, and to take action steps toward greater health, will take you on the path to your own wellness holy grail. And the second part of the grail journey, is to take it out into the world and let it bring healing to others. It is the next step of our journey; it's where the miracles really start showing up. This is an integral part of our Empowered Life Plan. First, we initiate emotional health, nutrition, and spiritual wellness into our lives, and then we find a place to help and make a difference in the world at large. This is what leads to a powerful journey and the most potent of lasting legacies. Our contribution in the world can be a strong force for good. It can affect one person indelibly, or it can be wider, grander, and greater than we often can imagine. This is living an empowered life of balanced wellness.

Helping people to visualize positive health outcomes and real transformation is a huge focus of my message and my work. Putting positive steps into real, consistent, sustained action sets us free, allows love to flow in, and creates in us a greater wellness to be realized.

Without love, we would be unable to experience freedom or wellness. Being free is the result of, and combination of, love and wellness. And of course, wellness is the integration of love and its resulting freedom. They are indelibly linked together in the very essence of our being.

Questions to Ponder

Chapter Seven

"In Chinese, the word for heart and mind is the same - Hsin.
For when the heart is open and the mind is clear, they are of one
substance, of one essence."
—Stephen Levine, *Who Dies? An Investigation of Conscious
Living and Conscious Dying*

Below you'll find questions that are meant to help you clarify for yourself
where you are at, in order for you to take a personal inventory of your life
and your future growth.

These questions are for the deep exploration of the places where love,
freedom, and wellness may be struggling to burst forth within you. Be
honest with yourself. The truth can be uncomfortable to face, but it can
also save your life and ultimately set you free. If crucial aspects remain
unresolved in you, they will affect all other areas of your life, health, and
spirit. Internal questioning is the key to understanding, healing, and
becoming whole. All the answers are within you.

Psychological Wellness:

1. Are you dealing with something in your life that you never thought
you would?

_____

2. Do you feel your life is a paradox in some ways?

_____

3. Do you treat yourself with respect? Do you treat others with respect?

_____

4. Do you feel worthy or unworthy of goodness?

_____

5. Do you feel it is time to learn from your life challenges and transform?

_____

6. Are you able to see your positive qualities and your difficulties in a balance inside of you?

_____

7. How does your inner voice speak to you? Are you kind and supportive to yourself in a constructive way? Or are you highly critical of yourself, and verbally beat yourself up?

_____

8. Have you made poor decisions that have led to much suffering both for you and others?

_____

9. Do you feel empty?

_____

10. Are you anxious, depressed, or in despair?

_____

11. How is your communication with others? What is your biggest challenge with communication? Are you able to put into words what is truly in your heart?

---

12. Does a constant need for validation make you easily seduceable, or vulnerable to being manipulated and taken advantage of?

---

13. Do you look for fulfillment and validation in unhealthy places or self-destructive behaviors?

---

14. Are you addicted to a person, or group, that is not good for you?

---

15. Are you afraid to step out of this behavior for fear of what they will think about you?

---

16. Do you drink and drive or allow others to drink and drive?

---

17. Are you using substances or behaviors that you know are destructive to you that you would not want others to find out about?

---

18. Do your significant other, your family, your friends, and your co-workers, feel that you listen to them and really hear them?

---

19. Do you ever say you are sorry with true meaning and a willingness to see your part and change your behavior?

_____

20. Are you afraid of emotional intimacy?

_____

21. Do you feel guilty about something and are unresolved about it?

_____

22. Do you have deep shame hidden inside you that you punish yourself for?

_____

23. Do you realize that reaching out for help is a sign of strength not weakness?

_____

24. Do you set healthy boundaries for yourself?

_____

25. Do you hold yourself, and others, accountable for decisions and actions?

_____

26. Do you feel compelled to please others no matter what, even if it is self-destructive?

_____

27. Are you with someone who has narcissistic qualities?

_____

28. If so, how does this affect you?

_____

29. Are you in a relationship where if you bring up your true concerns, the other person gets angry and tries to shut you down.

_____

30. What would you like to accomplish now and in the next five years?

_____

Nutritional Wellness:

1. How is your health?

_____

2. How would you like your health to improve?

_____

3. Are you troubled about your health and have not, as of yet, gotten the answers that you need?

_____

4. Do you feel it is possible for your health to improve?

_____

5. Has a doctor ever asked you about what you eat, and inquired about real details of your health practices?

_____

6. Are you confused about where and how to start improving your health?

_____

7. How is your self-care? What specifically are the challenges with your self-care and the areas you need to improve?

_____

8. Do you find yourself always hungry?

_____

9. Are you addicted to sugar?

_____

10. Do you avoid artificial sweeteners?

_____

11. Are you willing to research the impact that GMOs, pesticide, heavy metals, and preservatives in the food you eat have on your body?

_____

12. Do you notice what foods do not agree with you, through reactions and symptoms that you experience?

_____

13. Are you willing to be open to powerful solutions?

_____

14. Do you want greater energy, vitality, and longevity?

_____

15. Do you want to eat well, but do not know how to incorporate eating well into your life, no matter what information you know about?

_____

16. Are you self-destructive in the area of eating?

_____

17. Do you plan so that you actually have something healthy and pleasing to eat, when you are hungry?

_____

18. How is your energy?

_____

19. Is good health and nutrition important to you?

_____

20. How do you sleep?

_____

21. Do you snore?

_____

22. Have you had your snoring evaluated?

_____

23. Are you tired when you wake up in the morning?

_____

24. How much coffee do you drink?

_____

25. Do you use coffee to combat your fatigue?

_____

26. Do you know about adrenal fatigue, and its signs, symptoms, and that there are solutions?

_____

27. Are there conditions you have that you want to eliminate, which require living a healthier lifestyle?

_____

28. Are you able to integrate a healthier lifestyle consistently?

_____

29. How do you feel about your body? Are you in conflict?

_____

30. Are you willing to never give up getting the healing and answers you need?

_____

Spiritual Wellness:
1. What do you believe in?

_____

2. Are you able to put into words what is truly in your heart and soul?

_____

3. Do you feel true compassion for others? Do you have compassion for yourself?

_____

4. Does your intuition serve you?

_____

5. Are you drawn to developing your intuition and spirituality?

_____

6. Do you have an inner emotional/spiritual home to go to?

_____

7. Do you feel connected to your true self?

_____

8. Do you honor your true self?

_____

9. Have you found your meaning and purpose?

_____

10. What inspires you? What gives you hope?

_____

11. Who has inspired you the most in your life?

_____

12. What are the deepest truths that you have learned?

_____

13. What do you truly need now, and are searching for?

_____

14. What is really hurting you that is limiting your healing on all levels of your being?

_____

15. What do you believe about yourself that cuts you short in your own eyes?

_____

16. Do you limit what is possible for you, instead of realizing what is vast and eternal in you?

_____

17. Do you see and hold your value within?

_____

18. Do you feel loveable?

_____

19. Do you feel loved?

_____

20. What can you do to create something different, something that you truly want?

_____

21. Who would you like to help?

_____

22. What touches your heart?

_____

23. What have you noticed in the world that needs change and a new approach?

_____

24. What are your dreams about helping, being part of something meaningful that you could put into action?

_____

25. What are the most important moments of your life? The most poignant? The most touching?

_____

26. Do you feel in union with your higher self and higher purpose in life?

_____

27. Do you feel emptiness inside?

_____

28. What are you filling your emptiness with?

_____

29. Similar to the food we fill our bodies with, what are you really hungry for in your deepest being?

_____

30. What is your spiritual mystery that you are longing to find out?

_____

In my experience as a long time therapist, people do not get over deep hurts easily, unless some real work has been done to heal enough to go forward with our lives. There are some hurts that we will never get over, but there are some scars that may soften in time, and we learn to live with them. We need compassion for ourselves, for what is unhealed in us. There is a way through.

Empowered Life Plan:
Getting Started Wherever You Are

Chapter Eight

We are what we drink
We are what we eat
We are what we think
We are what we believe
Time to wake up!

The Four Truths of Wellness:

- We need health, resilience, vibrancy, and strength, to meet the challenges of our lives.
- We need to create positive changes, and become in tune with what our body, mind, and soul need.
- We have the power to do something about whatever health and life challenges we are dealing with.
- Our attitude and belief colors our lives every second of the day, and reflects in our self-care and in the choices we make.

Part One: Water

How much water do you drink each day? Are you hydrated? Are you dehydrated? The symptoms of dehydration are thirst, headaches, dry skin, dry eyes, low urine output, muscle cramps, and fatigue. Many people are chronically dehydrated and have some of these symptoms, but do not realize that they are suffering from not drinking enough water.

You can calculate how much water you need, by dividing your body weight in half. So, if you weigh 200 pounds, you need 100 ounces of water a day. Observe how much better you feel when you are more hydrated.

Drink the purest water possible, avoiding plastic containers with BPA. Start your day with hot or room temperature water mixed with a few teaspoons of fresh lemon juice. It's a great detoxifier for the liver, it's alkaline forming, and can stimulate peristalsis (the elimination process).

Part Two: Sleep

"My bed is a magical place, that when I get in it I remember all the things I was supposed to do, and all the things I am worried about."
—Unknown

What is quality of your sleep? How can you improve your sleep? Does your mind chatter away when you are trying to rest? Do you snore, or sleep next to someone who snores and disturbs your sleep? Is the person in your life who snores willing to get help with their snoring? Nothing takes the place of good quality sleep, and it is a major key to our wellness plan. Even if we do not have sleep apnea, snoring can have serious health effects.

Some factors affecting good quality sleep:
A. **Dairy:** People who eat dairy are often congested, which makes snoring worse. They may also have post-nasal drip, colds, bronchitis, or sinus infections, which all affect sleep quality. Chronic congestion is a serious symptom that can be cleared up by avoiding dairy foods.

B. **Sugar and Processed Food:** These can disrupt neurotransmitters, and unbalanced blood sugar can interfere with good sleep.

C. **Alcohol:** Alcohol can greatly impact our sleep in a negative way, causing alcohol-induced insomnia. Many people suffer from this especially after over-drinking. They might fall asleep, but they keep waking up with disturbed sleep, dry mouth, brain irritability, and dehydration. What is really going on in your body when you are "hung over?" It is your body being overwhelmed by the liver and brain toxicity of excess alcohol. Usually the next day is wasted by not feeling well, and trying to recover from your agony. Is this happening to you, or to someone you love?

D. **Stress:** Managing stress is essential for quality sleep and to balance our nervous system's health. Are your adrenals in balance? Our cortisol levels are supposed to be lowest at night and highest in the morning. If cortisol is elevated at night, it can interfere with sleep. If we have adrenal fatigue, we can sleep all night and still wake up feeling exhausted and low energy. This symptom needs attention and evaluation.

E. **Sleep Hygiene:** Using cell phones, computers, and watching disturbing or violent programs before sleep stimulates your brain, creating excitable brain chemistry. Instead, we need to give our body and brain a calming and soothing preparation for deep relaxation and high quality sleep, so turn off those devices!

F. **Hormonal Imbalance:** Hormonal balance is very important for deep restful sleep. Please have your hormones checked by an integrative doctor to see if you have hormonal imbalances.

Symptoms of hormonal imbalance are:
   In women: PMS, fibroids, sleep issues, low sex drive, fatigue, hot flashes, weight gain around the middle, anxiety, headaches, irritability, memory problems, fogginess, and depression.

In men: muscle loss, weight gain around the middle, fatigue, sleep problems, lower sex drive, ED, hair loss, urinary problems, and memory loss.

G. Consuming Excess Caffeine: Many people drink more coffee than water, and are dehydrated and racing from the caffeine. This can interfere with their sleep.

Part Three: The Eating Continuum
- First contemplate what to avoid or eliminate in your diet.
- Take one step at a time and do not get overwhelmed.
- Allow yourself time to adjust to the changes.

AVOID LIST:
- Dairy
- Processed and fast foods
- Denatured food
- White flour
- Gluten, as much as possible
- Bromide flour
- Sugar in its many forms (Instead you can use Stevia or Xylitol)
- High fructose corn syrup, and regular corn syrup
- Carrageenan
- Deep fried foods
- All trans fats and hydrogenated fats
- Poor quality oils like, canola, cottonseed oil, corn oil, safflower oil, sunflower oil, vegetable oil, and soybean oil
- GMO food
- Factory-farmed and processed meat, fish, and eggs
- Non-organic agriculture. Avoid these as much as possible, as they

may contain high levels of pesticides and heavy metals.
• Artificial Sweeteners

INCLUDE LIST:

• *Increase plant-based proteins that have high nutrition:* Beans, nuts, nut butters, nut milks, seeds (chia, sesame, tahini, hemp, sunflower), almonds, brazil nuts, avocadoes, quinoa, spirulina, chlorella, wheatgrass juice, and sprouts (mung beans, lentils, pea sprouts, sunflower greens).

• *Organic fruits and vegetables:* 9-13 servings a day.

• *Abundant greens:* kale, collard greens, wheatgrass, broccoli, and many more.

• *Green sprouts:* pea, sunflower greens, broccoli, micro greens, and sprouted mung beans

• *Beans:* lentils, garbanzo beans, chickpeas (use in soups, patés, hummus, veggie-burgers, and more).

• *Healthy fats:* From whole food sources, such as: avocados, seeds, nuts, and nut butters.

• *Raw organic nuts and seeds:* sunflower, chia, flax, sesame, hemp, almonds, almond milk, sesame tahini, walnuts, and pine nuts. (You can use any of these soaked for a creamy base for soups, dips, and desserts.) We do not need milk-based foods for creaminess! Please step outside of the box, and stop being brainwashed! Chia seed pudding is sooo good, and great for you. It's a great replacement for yogurt and the desire for creaminess.

• *Non-fish omega-3s:* They can prevent you from ingesting all of the toxins that, sadly, the oceans now contain. Algae-based omega-3s, such as flax oil, flax seeds, walnuts, pumpkin seeds, and hemp seeds.

• *Avocados:* They are high in potassium, minerals, and nutrients. You can make dressings, guacamole with jicama (crunchy and sweet) to dip into. Try asking for raw veggies or jicama in Mexican restaurants to dip into your guacamole instead of deep fried corn chips!

• *Organic green juices and smoothies*
• *Include superfoods in your diet:* chlorella, high chlorophyll foods, spirulina, sunflower sprouts, berries, wheatgrass, maca, chia seeds, flax seeds, hemp seeds, and sea vegetables. (Make sure the ones you use, are organic, toxin-free, and the finest quality.)
• *Whole grains:* 2 servings per day. Gluten-free whole grains (if they agree with you), such as: millet, amaranth, brown rice, quinoa, barley, buckwheat, steel cut oats, and wild rice.
• *Herbs and spices:* Seasoning your food with the following spices and herbs can add not only great taste, but offers health benefits as well:

Anise Seeds	Good source calcium and fiber, helps calm upset stomach
Basil	Anti-inflammatory, antibacterial properties
Dill	Contains iron and calcium; its oils may help neutralize carcinogens
Cilantro	Good source of phytonutrients, fiber, and iron
Cinnamon	Anti-inflammatory and antibiotic properties, helps relieve arthritis stiffness
Cloves	Highest in antioxidants
Coriander	May help control blood sugar, cholesterol and free radical production
Cumin	May help people with diabetes keep blood sugar levels in check. Germ fighting principles
Fennel	An aid in fighting bloating, gas, heartburn
Garlic	Anti-inflammatory, cardiovascular benefits, cancer protection

Ginger	Anti-inflammatory, immune system booster, cardiovascular benefits
Jamaican Allspice	Gut health, blood sugar control
Lavender	Helps ease stress and promote sleep
Marjoram	Aids digestion, relieves stress
Mint	Helps with alleviating symptoms of irritable bowel syndrome
Nutmeg	Fights bacteria and fungi
Oregano	Antioxidant with strong broad-spectrum antibiotic and antifungal properties
Parsley	Heart healthy folate and vitamins K, C, and A
Rosemary	May increase circulation and improve digestion
Sage	Anti-inflammatory, anti-oxidant
Thyme	Helps infections heal faster, protects cell membranes
Turmeric	Protective against cancer and Alzheimer's

There are many wonderful recipes available that can delight your palette, and nourish and honor your body. As you incorporate these life-giving foods, they will become a natural part of your life every day.

Part Four: Detoxification

Love your liver! It is important to have adequate antioxidants from whole food fruits, vegetables, and berries to protect the body from harm from free radicals and potent toxins, that if not neutralized, can impact our bodies negatively.

Engage all the naturally built-in systems in your body for detoxification:

perspiration (you can use exercise or infrared saunas), hydration, urination, healthy elimination, lymphatic detoxification, dry skin brushing, rebounding, skin detoxification, green organic juices, having a pure diet, avoiding smoking, drugs, over-drinking and exposure to chemicals, pesticides, deep fried foods, trans fats, bad oils, and fast foods.

Part Five: Movement

Exercise your freedom to move! Do something each day to love and honor your body through movement. At least 30 minutes, 3x a week. Include weight resistance training and cardio.

There are so many options to choose from! Just find one you enjoy and commit to it. Choose to begin a movement plan today, and become consistent with your activity. Your body will soon crave the exercise, and this will work to reduce stress and prevent sarcopenia (the loss of muscle mass which accelerates aging).

Part Six: Adrenal Support

Make a stress management plan to support your adrenals:
1. Get a massage
2. Schedule in some down time with peace and quiet every day
3. Make time to laugh and enjoy yourself every day
4. Try meditation and/or guided visualizations
5. Listen to meditative music
6. Seek out healing modalities, such as Reiki, Therapeutic Touch, and others.

Part Seven: Self-Empowerment

Take one day at a time. Simply making one significant change in your life will help lead to the next one, and will give you the confidence to keep going:

1. Learn to keep in positive harmony with yourself.
2. Clarify and focus on your goals for your health.
3. Reach out for the support needed to achieve your goals.
4. Continue working through your challenges and give attention to your personal growth.
5. Become empowered in your process of growing so you can become who you truly are.
6. Never give up! There are gifts and teachings waiting for you on your journey of healing body, mind, and soul.
7. Realize the power of your free will in choosing your health lifestyle. Choosing to commit to your health and self-care will grace your life in numerous ways, as you begin to honor your body.
8. When you climb the mountain of possibility, you only can see how far you have come when you look back. It is so uplifting when you realize that your whole life you have made excellent choices that have helped you. Realize and acknowledge the wisdom you have gained from overcoming adversity.
9. Choose to put love and care into you and your health.

Bibliography

Amen, Daniel M.D. *Healing ADD*. New York: Berkeley Pub Group, 2001.

Beattie, Melody. *Codependent No More*. Center City, MN: Hazelden, 1992.

Blaylock, Russell M.D. *Excitotoxins*. Santa Fe: Health Press, 1997.

Brogaard, Berit. "How Does High Cortisol Affect the Amygdala?" http://www.livestrong.com/article/174446-how-does-high-cortisol-affect-the amygdala. Accessed December12, 2013.

Bradshaw, John. *Bradshaw on The Family*. Deerfield Beach: Health Communications, 1996.

--. *Healing The Shame That Binds You*. Deerfield Beach: Health Communications, 2005.

Butterworth, Eric. *Discover The Power Within You*. New York: Harper Collins, 1989.

Campbell, Colin. *The China Study*. Dallas: Ben Bella Books, 2005.

Carlebach, Shlomo. *Shlomo's Stories*. Lanhan: Roman and Littlefield Pub, 1994.

Carnes, Patrick Ph.D. *Out of the Shadows*. Center City: Hazelden, 2001.

Chopra, Deepak M.D. and Rudolph E. Tanzi, Ph.D. "Radical Well-Being, Where We Need To Go." Huffington Post. http://www.huffingtonpost.com/deepak-chopra/radical-wellbeing-where-w_b_4804118.html (February 19, 2014)

Clement, Anna Maria. *Healthful Cuisine*. Juno Beach, FL: Healthful Communications, Inc, 2007.

Clement, Brian. *Hippocrates Life Force*. Summertown, TN: Healthy Living Pub, 2007.

Crary, Robert Wall. *The Still Small Voice*. Cleveland: Risshis Institute of Metaphysics, 1986.

Dass, Ram. *Be Love Now: The Path of the Heart*. New York: Harper Collins, 2010.

Dass, Ram and Paul Gorman. *How Can I Help?* New York: Alfred A. Knopf Inc., 1985.

Ekman, Paul and Wallace Friesen. *Unmasking the Face*. Los Altos: Malor Books, 2003.

Forward, Susan. *Men Who Hate Women and The Women Who Love Them*. New York: Bantam Books, 1987.

Frankl, Viktor M.D., Ph.D. *Man's Search for Meaning*. Boston: Beacon Press Books, 2006.

--. *The Will to Meaning*. New York: Penguin Books, 1988.

Harvard Health Publications. "Teenage Drinking: Understanding The Dangers and Talkin to Your Child." Accessed February 4, 2014. http://www.helpguide.org.

Hesse, Hermann. *Siddhartha*. New York: New Directions Pub and Bantam, 1951.

Holmes, Earnest. *How to Use the Science of Mind*. Los Angeles: Science of Mind Pub, 2002.

--. *Thoughts Are Things*. Deerfield Beach: Science of Mind Pub, 1999.

Houston, Mark M.D. *What Your Doctor May Not Tell You About Heart Disease*. New York: Grand Central Life & Style, 2012.

Jones, David, et al. *Textbook of Functional Medicine*. Gig Harbor, WA: Institute of Functional Medicine, 2006. 116, 195, 196, 543–580.

Jung, Carl. *Psychological Reflections: An Anthology of the Writings of C. G. Jung*. Michigan: Harper, 1961.

Kabat-Zinn, Jon. *Wherever You Go, There You Are*. New York: Hyperion, 1994.

Kubler-Ross, Elisabeth. *On Death and Dying*. New York: Scribner Classics, 1997.

Levine, Stephen. *A Gradual Awakening*. New York: Anchor Books, 1989.

Life Extension Foundation. "Aging and Inflammation." Accessed August 27, 2009. http://www.lef.org/protocols/prtcl-146.shtml.

--. "Asthma Updated". Accessed August 27, 2009. http://www.lef.org/LEFcms/.aspx/PrintVersionMagic.aspx.?cmsID=113916.

--. "Coronary Artery Disease and Atherosclerosis." Accessed August 27, 2009. http://www.lef.org/LEFcms/.aspx/PrintVersionMagic.aspx?cmsID=113979

Lipton, Bruce. *The Biology of Belief*. Carlsbad, CA: Hay House, 2007

McLeod, S.A. "Defense Mechanisms." Accessed July 15, 2012. http://www.simplypsychology.org/defensemechanisms/html.

Murphy, Joseph. *The Power of Your Subconscious Mind*. Englewood Cliffs: Prentice Hall, 1963.

Nakken, Craig. *The Addictive Personality*. Center City, MN: Hazelden, 1996.

Norwood, Robin. *Women Who Love Too Much*. New York: Pocket Books, 1985.

Perkins, Russell. *The Impact of a Saint*. New Hampshire: The Sant Bani Press, 1980.

Sharma, Robin S. *The Monk Who Sold His Ferrari*. New York: Harper Collins, 1997.

Siegel, Bernie. *Love, Medicine, and Miracles*. New York: Harper Perennial, 1990.

Sinatra, Stephen M.D. *Metabolic Cardiology*. Laguna Beach: Basic Health Publications, 2005.

Tracy, Brian. *Focal Point*. New York: Amacom Books, 2002.

Wegschieder-Cruse, Sharon. *The Miracle of Recovery.* Rapid City: On Site Training and Consulting Inc., 1989.

Wigmore, Ann. *Be Your Own Doctor.* Wayne, NJ: Avery Publishing, 1982.

Wilson, James. *Adrenal Fatigue.* Petaluma: Smart Publications, 2001.

Wright, Jonathan M.D. and Lane Lenard Ph.D. *Stay Young and Sexy with Bioidentical Hormone Replacement.* Petaluma: Smart Publications, 2010.

Yogananda, Paramahansa. *Autobiography of a Yogi.* Los Angeles: Self Realization Fellowship, 2007.

--. *Where There Is Light.* Los Angeles: Self Realization Fellowship, 1988.

Aml
5/14

CPSIA information can be obtained at www.ICGtesting.com
Printed in the USA
BVOW04s1634140414

350610BV00018B/1078/P